EASY GUITAR

THE Early Rock BOOK

T5-CGA-877

ISBN 0-634-04492-3

HAL•LEONARD®
CORPORATION

7777 W. BLUEMOUND RD. P.O. BOX 13819 MILWAUKEE, WI 53213

Visit Hal Leonard Online at
www.halleonard.com

THE Early Rock BOOK

STRUM AND PICK PATTERNS

This chart contains the suggested strum and pick patterns that are referred to by number at the beginning of each song in this book. The symbols ⊓ and ∨ in the strum patterns refer to down and up strokes, respectively. The letters in the pick patterns indicate which right-hand fingers plays which strings.

p = thumb
i = index finger
m = middle finger
a = ring finger

For example; Pick Pattern 2
is played: thumb - index - middle - ring

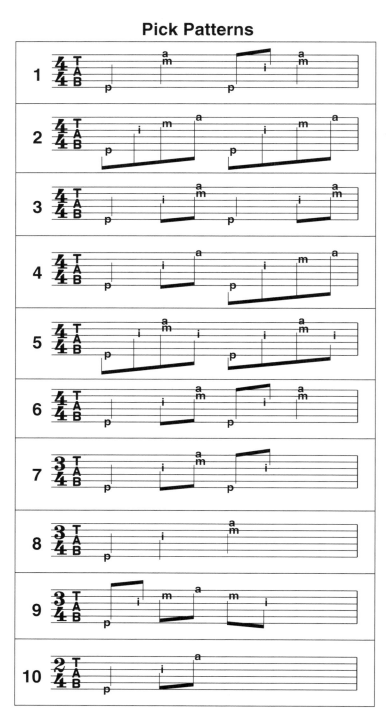

Strum Patterns   ## Pick Patterns

You can use the 3/4 Strum or Pick Patterns in songs written in compound meter (6/8, 9/8, 12/8, etc.).
For example, you can accompany a song in 6/8 by playing the 3/4 pattern twice in each measure.
The 4/4 Strum and Pick Patterns can be used for songs written in cut time (¢) by doubling the note time values in the patterns. Each pattern would therefore last two measures in cut time.

All Shook Up

Words and Music by Otis Blackwell and Elvis Presley

Outro

my hand, what a chill I got. Her lips are like __ a vol -

ca - no that's hot! I'm __ proud to say that she's my but - ter - cup. I'm in

love! I'm all shook up. __ Mm, _ mm, ooh, ooh, yeah, _

1. yeah, __ yeah! __ My __ yeah, __ yeah! __ Mm, _

mm, ooh, ooh, yeah, __ yeah, __ I'm all shook up!

Additional Lyrics

2. A-well, my hands are shaky and my knees are weak,
I can't seem to stand on my own two feet.
Who do you thank when you have such luck?
I'm in love! I'm all shook up! Mm, mm, ooh, ooh, yeah, yeah, yeah!

Bridge My tongue gets tied when I try to speak.
My insides shake like a leaf on a tree.
There's only one cure for this soul of mine.
That's to have the girl that I love so fine!

Blue Suede Shoes
Words and Music by Carl Lee Perkins

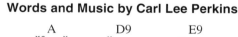

Strum Pattern: 6
Pick Pattern: 4

𝄋 **Verse**

Bright Country shuffle

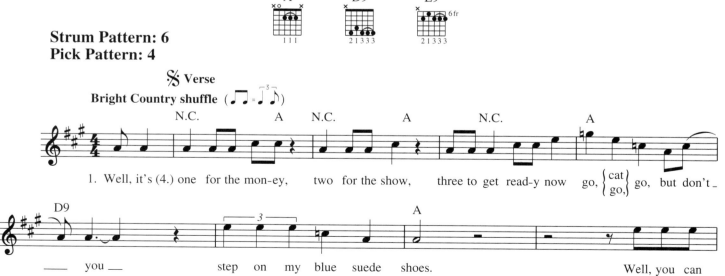

1. Well, it's (4.) one for the mon-ey, two for the show, three to get read-y now go, {cat go, go,} go, but don't __

__ you __ step on my blue suede shoes. Well, you can

All I Have to Do Is Dream

Words and Music by Boudleaux Bryant

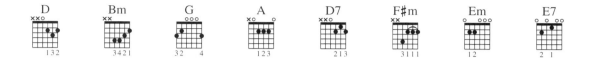

Intro
Moderately

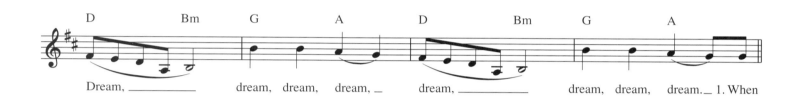

Dream, _____ dream, dream, dream, _ dream, _____ dream, dream, dream. _ 1. When

Verse

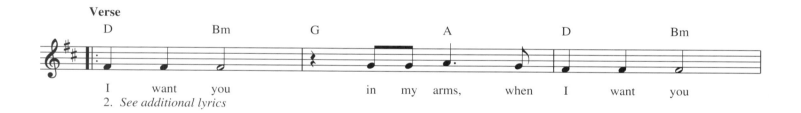

I want you in my arms, when I want you
2. *See additional lyrics*

and all your charms. When-ev-er I want you _ all I have to do is

dream, _____ dream, dream, dream. 2. When dream. _____

Bridge

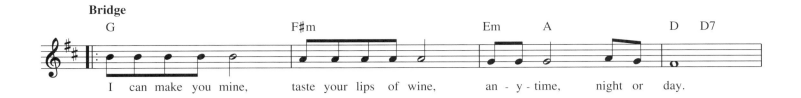

I can make you mine, taste your lips of wine, an-y-time, night or day.

On-ly trou-ble is, gee whiz, I'm dream-ing my life ___ a - way! ___ 3., 4. I

Verse

need you so that I could die, I love you so

and that is why, when - ev - er I want you ___ all I have to do is

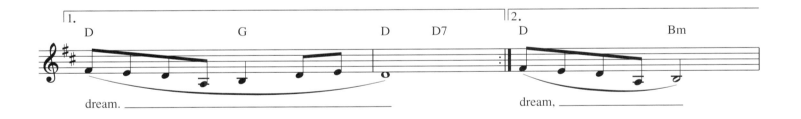

dream. ___   dream, ___

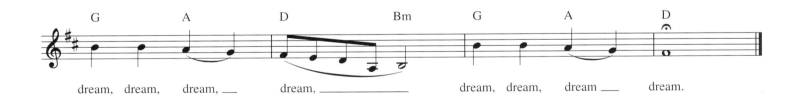

dream, dream, dream, ___ dream, ___ dream, dream, dream ___ dream.

Additional Lyrics

2. When I feel blue in the night,
   And I need you to hold me tight.
   Whenever I want you
   All I have to do is dream.

At the Hop

Words and Music by Arthur Singer, John Madara and David White

Strum Pattern: 2
Pick Pattern: 4

Additional Lyrics

2. Well, you can swing it, you can groove it,
   You can really start to move it at the hop.
   Where the jockey is the smoothest
   And the music is the coolest at the hop.
   All the cats and the chicks can get their kicks at the hop.

4. You can swing it, you can groove it,
   You can really start to move it at the hop.
   Where the jockey is the smoothest
   And the music is the coolest at the hop.
   All the cats and the chicks can get their kicks at the hop.
   Spoken: Let's go!

Baby Love

Words and Music by Brian Holland, Edward Holland and Lamont Dozier

Strum Pattern: 3
Pick Pattern: 3

Verse

Moderately

1. Ba - by love, my ba - by love, I need you, oh, how I need _ you.
2., 3. *See additional lyrics*

But all you do is treat me bad, _____ break my heart and leave me sad. _____

Wan-na know what did I do wrong _ to make you stay a - way so long. 'Cause ba-by love, my

ba - by love, been miss-ing ya, miss _ kiss-ing ya. In - stead of break-ing up, _____

let's start some kiss-ing and mak-ing up. _____ Don't throw our love a - way. _____

1. In my arms why don't you stay?
2. got the best of

D.C. al Coda

Coda

hurt me, till it

Outro   *Repeat and fade*

hurt me. Ooh, _____ ba - by love, { don't / Don't } throw our love a - way.

Additional Lyrics

2. Baby love, my baby love, why must we separate my love?
All of my whole life through, I never love no one but you.
Why you do me like you do, I guess it's me, ooh.
Need to hold you once again my love, feel your warm embrace my love.
Don't throw our love away, please don't do me this way.
Not happy like I used to be. Loneliness has got the best of

3. Me my love, my baby love, I need ya, oh, how I need ya.
Why you do me like you do, after I've been true to you.
So deep in love with you. Baby, baby, ooh.
Till it hurt me, till it hurt me.
Ooh, baby love, don't throw our love a-way.

Barbara Ann

Words and Music by Fred Fassert

Be-Bop-A-Lula

Words and Music Tex Davis and Gene Vincent

Strum Pattern: 3
Pick Pattern: 3

Chorus
Moderately slow Rock

Be - bop - a - lu - la, she's my ba - by. Be - bop - a - lu - la, I don't mean may - be.

Be - bop - a - lu - la, she's my ba - by. Be - bop - a - lu - la, I don't mean may - be.

Be - bop - a - lu - la, she's my ba - by doll, my ba - by doll, my ba - by doll.

Verse

1. She's the gal in the red blue jeans. She's the queen of all the teens.
2. See additional lyrics

She's the one ___ that I know. She's the one that loves me so.

Outro

Be - bop - a - lu - la, she's my ba - by. Be - bop - a - lu - la, I don't mean may - be.

Be - bop - a - lu - la, she's my ba - by doll, my ba - by doll, my ba - by doll. doll.

Additional Lyrics

2. She's the one that's got the beat.
   She's the one with the flyin' feet.
   She's the one that walks around the store.
   She's the one that gets more and more.

Blueberry Hill

Words and Music by Al Lewis, Larry Stock and Vincent Rose

Strum Pattern: 2
Pick Pattern: 4

Additional Lyrics

2. The moon stood still
   On Blueberry Hill,
   And lingered until
   My dreams came true.

Big Girls Don't Cry

Words and Music by Bob Crewe and Bob Gaudio

Strum Pattern: 3
Pick Pattern: 3

Intro
Moderately

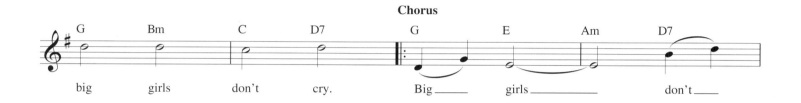

Big girls don't cry,

Chorus

big girls don't cry. Big___ girls___ don't___

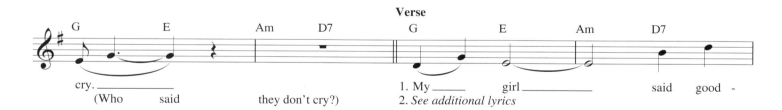

cry,___ they don't cry.___ Big___ girls___ don't___

Verse

cry.___ (Who said they don't cry?)   1. My___ girl___ said good -
2. *See additional lyrics*

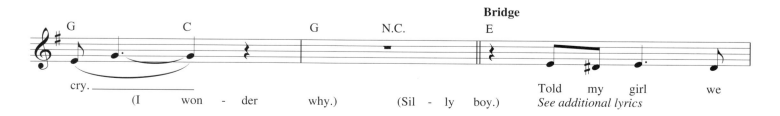

bye,___ my, oh my.___ My___ girl___ did - n't

Bridge

cry.___ (I won - der why.) (Sil - ly boy.) Told my girl we
See additional lyrics

had to break up, thought that she would call my bluff;

(Sil - ly boy.) (Sil - ly

Then she said to my sur - prise, ___ "Big girls

boy.)

Chorus

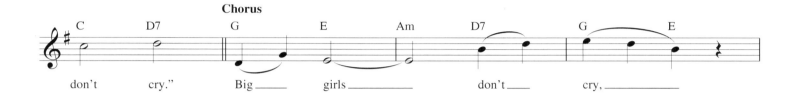

don't cry." Big ___ girls ___ don't ___ cry, ___

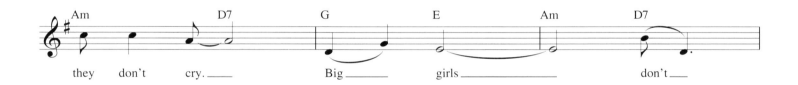

they don't cry. ___ Big ___ girls ___ don't ___

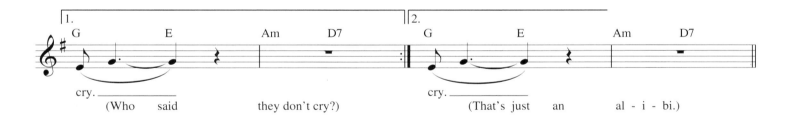

cry. (Who said they don't cry?) cry. ___ (That's just an al - i - bi.)

Outro

Big girls don't cry, big girls don't cry.

Additional Lyricss

2. Baby, I was true,
I was true.
Baby, I'm such a fool.
(I'm such a fool.)

Bridge (Silly girl.) Shame on you, your mama said,
(Silly girl.) Shame on you, you're cryin' in bed;
(Silly girl.) Shame on you, you told a lie.
Big girls don't cry.

Bird Dog

Words and Music by Boudleaux Bryant

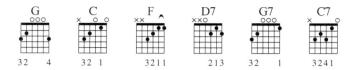

Strum Pattern: 1
Pick Pattern: 4

Intro
Moderately

Verse

1. John - ny is a jok - er,
2., 3. *See additional lyrics*

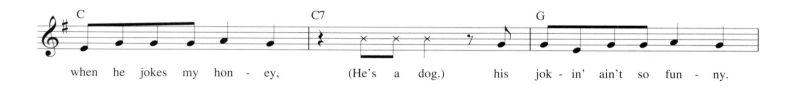

Spoken: (He's a bird.) a ver - y fun - ny jok - er. (He's a bird.) But

when he jokes my hon - ey, (He's a dog.) his jok - in' ain't so fun - ny.

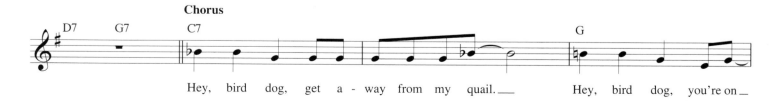

(What a dog.) John-ny is the jok - er that's a - try-in' to steal my ba - by. (He's a bird dog.)

Chorus

Hey, bird dog, get a - way from my quail.___ Hey, bird dog, you're on___

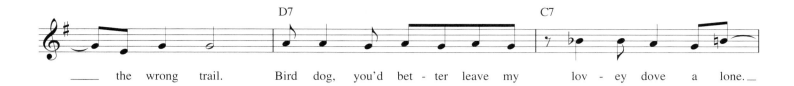

_____ the wrong trail. Bird dog, you'd bet - ter leave my lov - ey dove a lone. __

_____ Hey, bird dog, get a - way from my chick. __

Hey, bird dog, you'd bet - ter get a - way quick. __ Bird dog, you'd bet - ter find a

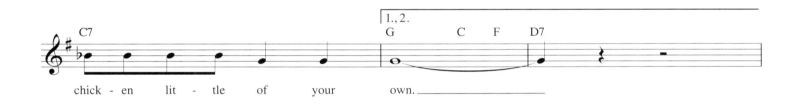

chick - en lit - tle of your own. _____

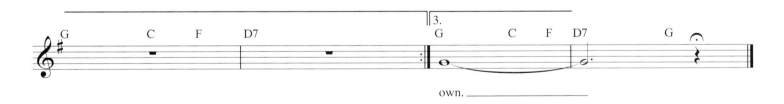

own. _____

Additional Lyrics

2. Johnny sings a love song, (Like a bird.)
He sings the sweetest love song. (You ever heard.)
But when he sings to my gal, (What a howl.)
To me he's just a wolf dog. (On the prowl.)
Johnny wants to fly away and puppy love my baby. (He's a bird dog.)

3. Johnny kissed the teacher; (He's a bird.)
He tiptoed up to reach her. (He's a bird.)
Well, he's the teacher's pet now; (He's a dog)
What he wants he can get now. (What a dog.)
He even made the teacher let him sit next to my baby. (He's a bird dog.)

Bo Diddley

Words and Music by Ellas McDaniel

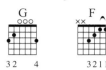

Strum Pattern: 6
Pick Pattern: 6

dia - mond ring. ___   If   that   dia - mond ring ___

___ don't shine, ___   he gon - na take it to a

pri - vate eye. ___   2. If   that   pri - vate

eye can't see,   he bet - ter not take the ring ___

___ from me.

Interlude

Play 4 times

Verse

3. Bo Did - dley caught a nan - ny goat _____ to
4. Bo Did - dley caught a bear - cat to

make his pret - ty ba - by a Sun - day coat. _
make his pret - ty ba - by a Sun - day hat. _

Verse

5. Won't ___ you come to my house and rack that bone, ___
6. Look at that ___ bo - do, oh, where's he been? ___

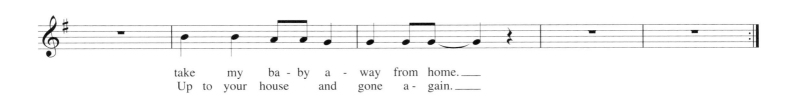

take my ba - by a - way from home. ___
Up to your house and gone a - gain. ___

Verse

7. Bo Did - dley, Bo Did - dley, have you heard? _____ My _

Outro

Repeat and fade

___ pret - ty ba - by said she was a bird. ___

Book of Love

Words and Music by Warren Davis, George Malone and Charles Patrick

Strum Pattern: 6
Pick Pattern: 6

1. Tell me, tell me, tell me, oh, who wrote the book of love? I've got to know the
2., 3. *See additional lyrics*

an-swer, was it some-one from a-bove? I won-der, won-der who,_____

who, who wrote the book of love? Chap-ter One says to

love her, to love her with all your heart. Chap-ter Two you tell her, you're

nev-er, nev-er, nev-er, nev-er, ev-er gon-na part. In Chap-ter Three re-mem-ber the

mean-ing of ro-mance. In Chap-ter Four you break up, but you give her just one more

chance. Oh, I won-der won-der who,_____ who,

who wrote the book of love?

love?_____

Additional Lyrics

2. I love you, darling,
Baby, you know I do.
But I've got to see this book of love,
Find out why it's true.

3. Baby, baby, baby,
I love you, yes, I do.
Well, it says so in this book of love,
Ours is the one that's true.

Bread and Butter

Words and Music by Larry Parks and Jay Turnbow

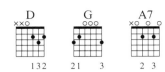

Strum Pattern: 3
Pick Pattern: 4

Verse

Moderate Rock

1. I like bread and but - ter. I like toast and jam.
2., 3. *See additional lyrics*

That's what my ba - by feeds me. I'm her lov - in' man.

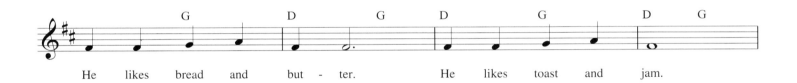

He likes bread and but - ter. He likes toast and jam.

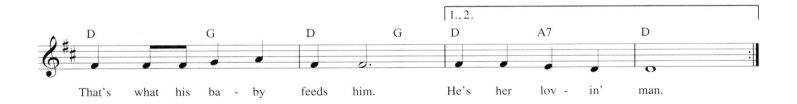

That's what his ba - by feeds him. He's her lov - in' man.

with some oth - er man.

Additional Lyrics

2. She don't cook mashed potatoes,
   Don't cook T-bone steak.
   Don't feed me peanut butter.
   She knows that I can't take
   No more bread and butter,
   No more toast and jam.
   He found his baby eatin'
   With some other man.

3. Got home early one mornin'
   Much to my surprise,
   She was eatin' chicken and dumplin's
   With some other guy.
   No more bread and butter,
   No more toast and jam.
   I found my baby eatin'
   With some other man.

Breaking Up Is Hard to Do

Words and Music by Howard Greenfield and Neil Sedaka

Bridge

do. They say that break-ing up is hard to do. Now I know, I

know that it's true. Don't say ___ that this is the end. ___

In - stead of break-ing up ___ I wish that we were mak - ing up a - gain,

Outro

I beg ___ of you, don't ___ say ___ good - bye. ___ Can't we give our love ___

___ a brand new try? ___ Yeah, ___ come on babe, ___ let's start a - new, 'cause

break - ing up is hard to do. ___ 3. Don't take your break - ing up is hard to do, ___

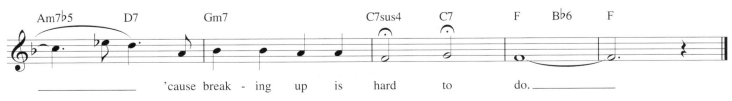

___ 'cause break - ing up is hard to do. ___

Bye Bye Love

Words and Music by Felice Bryant and Boudleaux Bryant

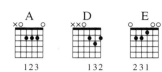

Strum Pattern: 2
Pick Pattern: 4

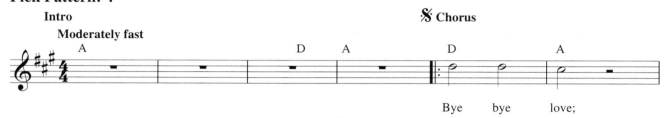

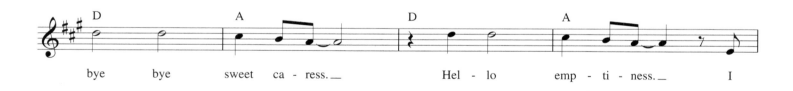

She sure looks hap - py, ___ I sure am blue. ___

She was my ba - by ___ till he stepped in; ___

good - bye to ro - mance ___ that might have been. ___

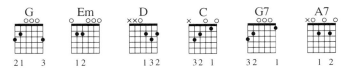

bye my love good - bye. Bye

Additional Lyrics

2. I'm through with romance, I'm through with love.
   I'm through with counting the stars above.
   And here's the reason that I'm so free;
   My lovin' baby is through with me.

Dream Lover

Words and Music by Bobby Darin

Strum Pattern: 2
Pick Pattern: 4

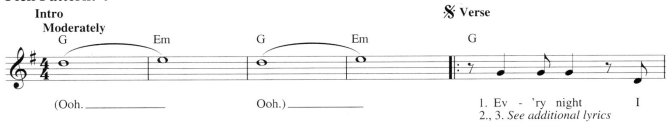

(Ooh. ___ Ooh.) ___ 1. Ev - 'ry night I
                                2., 3. *See additional lyrics*

hope and pray ___ a dream lov - er will come my way, ___ a girl to hold

in my arms___ and know the mag-ic of her charms. 'Cause I want a

girl to call__ my own,___ I want a dream_ lov-er so

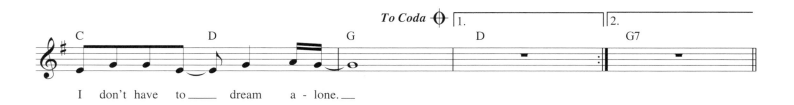

I don't have to__ dream a-lone.__

Some-day, I don't know how,__ I hope she'll a-hear my plea.__

Some-way, I don't know how,__ she'll bring her love to me.

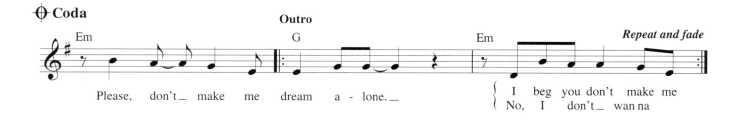

Please, don't_ make me dream a-lone.__

I beg you don't make me
No, I don't_ wan na

Additional Lyrics

2. Dream lover, where are you,
   With a love, oh, so true,
   And the hand that I can hold
   To feel you near as I grow old?

3. Dream lover, until then
   I'll go to sleep and dream again.
   That's the only thing to do
   Till all my lover's dreams come true.

Can't Help Falling in Love

from the Paramount Picture BLUE HAWAII

Words and Music by George David Weiss, Hugo Peretti and Luigi Creatore

Strum Pattern: 2
Pick Pattern: 4

Additional Lyrics

2. Shall I stay?
   Would it be a sin
   If I can't help falling in love with you?

Catch a Wave

Words and Music by Brian Wilson and Mike Love

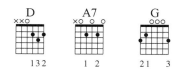

Strum Pattern: 2, 3
Pick Pattern: 5, 6

Verse
Moderately fast

1. Throw me a fa - vor, try the great - est sport a - round.
2., 3. *See additional lyrics*

Ev - 'ry - bod - y tries it once. Those who don't just have to put it

down. You pad - dle out, turn a - round and raise, and ba - by,

that's all there is to the coast - line craze. You got - ta catch a wave, and you're

sit - tin' on top of the world.

Additional Lyrics

2. Not just a fad 'cause it's been going on so long.
   All the surfers going strong; they said it wouldn't last too long.
   They'll eat their words with a fork and spoon, and watch 'em,
   They'll hit the road and be surfin' soon.
   And when they catch a wave, they'll be sitting on top of the world.

3. So take a lesson from a top notch surfer boy:
   Ev'ry Saturday, boy, but don't you treat it like a toy.
   Just get away from the shady turf, and baby,
   Go catch some rays on the sunny surf.
   And when you catch a wave, you'll be sitting on top of the world.

Chantilly Lace

Words and Music by J.P. Richardson

Strum Pattern: 2, 3
Pick Pattern: 3, 4

Intro — Freely

Verse — Moderately

Spoken: *Hello, baby.* 1. *Yeah, this is the Big Bopper speakin'. Ha, ha, ha, ha, ha, ha. Oh, you sweet thing!*
2., 3. *See additional lyrics*

Do I what? Will I what? Oh, baby, you know what I like!

Chorus

Chan - til - ly lace ___ and a pret - ty face ___ and a po - ny tail ___ a - hang - in' down, ___ a wig - gle in her walk and a gig - gle in her talk,

1., 3. make the world go 'round. ___
2. make the world go 'round. ___ round, round. ___

There ain't noth - in' in the world like a big - eyed girl ___ to make me act so fun - ny, make me spend my mon - ey, make me feel real loose like a long - necked goose, a - like a

1., 2. girl. *Oh, baby, that's-a what I like!*
3. girl. *Oh, baby, that's-a what I like!*

Additional Lyrics

2. Spoken: *What's that baby?*
But, but, but,
Oh, honey,
But, oh baby, you know what I like!

3. Spoken: *What's that honey?*
Pick you up at eight, and don't be late?
But, baby, I ain't got no money, honey!
Ha, ha, ha, ha, ha.
Oh, alright, honey, you know what I like!

Charlie Brown

Words and Music by Jerry Leiber and Mike Stoller

Donna

Words and Music by Ritchie Valens

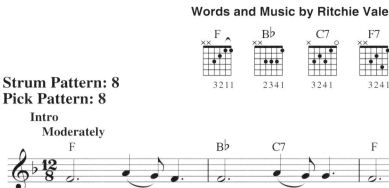

Strum Pattern: 8
Pick Pattern: 8

Intro
Moderately

Oh, Don - na, oh, Don - na, oh, Don - na, oh, Don - na.

Verse

1., 3. I had a girl, _____ Don - na _____ was her name, since she left me _____ I've

2. *See additional lyrics*

nev - er _____ been the same, _____ 'cause I love _____ my _ girl, _____ Don - na, _____ where _ can you

be, _____ where can _ you be? Don - na, _____ where _ can you be, _____ where _ can you

Bridge

be? _____ Oh, dar - lin' _____ now that you're gone _____ I don't know what I'll

D.S. al Coda
(take 1st ending)

do. All _____ my smiles _____ and all my love for _____ you. _____

Coda
Outro

Repeat and fade

Oh, Don - na, oh, Don - na, oh, Don - na, oh, Don - na.

Additional Lyrics

2. Now that you're gone, I'm left all alone,
   All by myself to wander and roam,
   'Cause I love you girl,
   Donna, where can you be,
   Where can you be?

Crying

Words and Music by Roy Orbison and Joe Melson

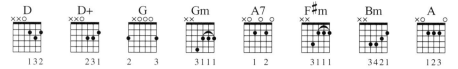

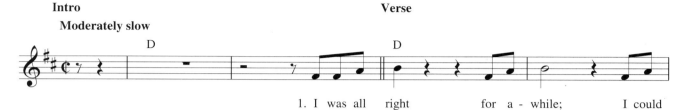

Strum Pattern: 2
Pick Pattern: 4

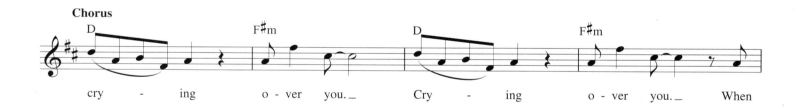

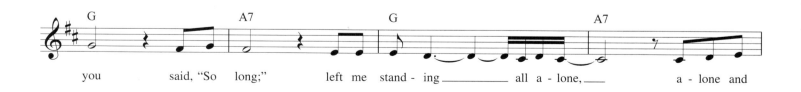

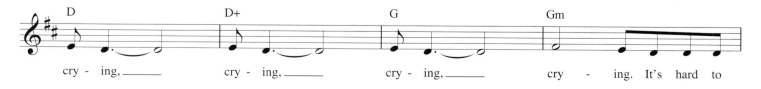

Dizzy Miss Lizzie

Words and Music by Larry Williams

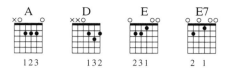

Strum Pattern: 1
Pick Pattern: 1

1. You make me diz - zy, Miss__ Liz - zie,_____ the way you rock and roll.__
2., 3. *See additional lyrics*

_____ You make me diz - zy, Miss__ Liz - zie,

when you do the Stroll._____ Come on, Miss Liz - zie,

love me 'fore I ___ grow too old. ___ Come on, ___ give me

Chorus

fe - ver, ___ put your lit - tle hand in mine. ___

You make me diz - zy, { Miss ___ / diz - zy } Liz - zie. Oh, girl, you look so

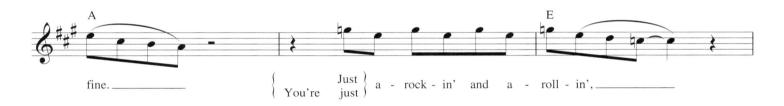

fine. ___ { You're / Just just } a - rock - in' and a - roll - in', ___

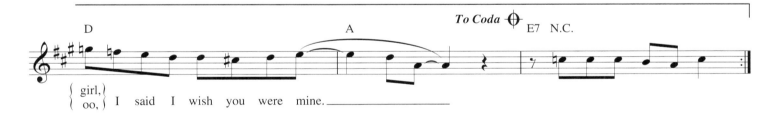

{ girl, / oo, } I said I wish you were mine. ___

man. ___

Additional Lyrics

2. You make me dizzy, Miss Lizzie,
   When you call my name.
   Woo, baby, say you're driving me insane.
   Come on, come on, come on, come on, baby,
   I wanna be your lovin' man.

3. Run and tell your mama
   I want you to be my bride.
   Run and tell your brother.
   Baby, don't run and hide.
   You make me dizzy, Miss Lizzie,
   Girl, I wanna marry you.

Do Wah Diddy Diddy

Words and Music by Jeff Barry and Ellie Greenwich

Strum Pattern: 2, 3
Pick Pattern: 2, 4

Additional Lyrics

3. Now we're together nearly ev'ry single day, singin',
   (Do wah diddy diddy dum diddy do.)
   We're so happy and that's how we're gonna stay, singin',
   (Do wah diddy diddy dum diddy do.)
   Well, I'm hers. (I'm hers.)
   She's mine. (She's mine.)
   I'm hers, she's mine.
   Wedding bells are gonna chime.

Don't Be Cruel
(To a Heart That's True)

Words and Music by Otis Blackwell and Elvis Presley

Strum Pattern: 6
Pick Pattern: 4

Intro

Moderate shuffle

Verse

Play 3 times

1. You know I can be found __
2. *See additional lyrics*

sit - ting home all a - lone. __ If you can't come a - round, __ at

least please tel - e - phone. __ Don't be cruel to a heart that's

1. true.

2. true. I don't

Bridge

want no oth - er love, __ ba - by it's just you I'm __ think - ing

Verse

of. __ 3. Don't stop think - ing of __ me, don't
4. *See additional lyrics*

make me feel this way. __ Come on o - ver here and love __ me, you

know what I want you to say. Don't be cruel to a heart that's

Bridge

true. Why should we be a - part? ____ I
See additional lyrics

1.

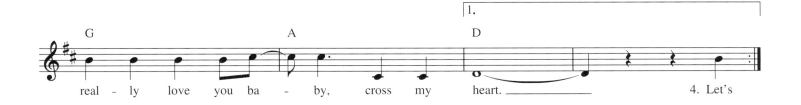

real - ly love you ba - by, cross my heart. _____ 4. Let's

2.

Outro

of. _____ Don't be cruel to a heart that's true. Don't be

cruel to a heart that's true. I don't want no oth - er love, _

____ ba - by it's just you I'm think-ing of.

Additional Lyrics

2. Baby, if I made you mad
   For something I might have said,
   Please let's forget the past,
   The future looks bright ahead.

4. Let's walk up to the preacher,
   And let us say, "I do."
   Then you'll know you'll have me,
   And I'll know that I have you.

Bridge I don't want no other love.
          Baby, it's just you I'm thinking of.

Duke of Earl

Words and Music by Earl Edwards, Eugene Dixon and Bernice Williams

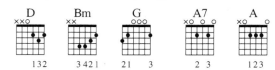

Strum Pattern: 1
Pick Pattern: 2

Additional Lyrics

2. When I hold you, you will be the Duchess of Earl.
   When I walk through my Dukedom, the paradise we will share.

Earth Angel

Words and Music by Jesse Belvin

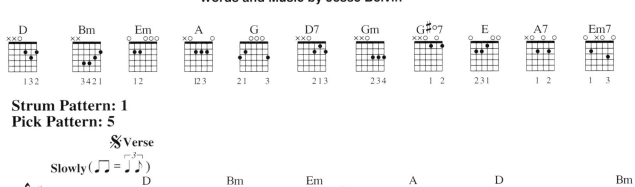

Strum Pattern: 1
Pick Pattern: 5

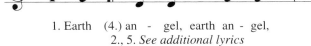

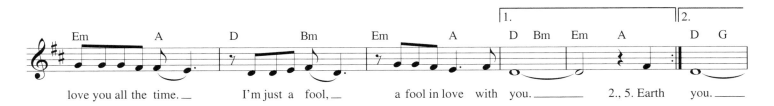

1. Earth (4.) an - gel, earth an - gel, will you be mine?___ My dar - ling, dear,___
2., 5. *See additional lyrics*

love you all the time. ___ I'm just a fool, ___ a fool in love with you. _____ 2., 5. Earth you. ___

Bridge

___ I fell for you, ___ and I knew the vi - sion of your love's love - li - ness. ___ I

hope and I pray ___ that some day ___ I'll be the vi - sion of your hap - pi - ness. 3., 6. Earth

Verse

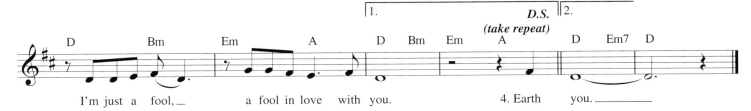

an - gel, earth an - gel, please be mine, ___ my dar - ling, dear, ___ love you all the time. ___

I'm just a fool, ___ a fool in love with you. 4. Earth you. _____

Additional Lyrics

2., 5. Earth angel, earth angel, the one I adore,
Love you forever and evermore.
I'm just a fool, a fool in love with you.

Fun, Fun, Fun

Words and Music by Brian Wilson and Mike Love

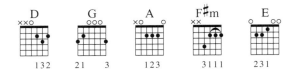

Strum Pattern: 2
Pick Pattern: 4

%· **Verse**

Bright Rock

1. Well, she got her dad-dy's car and she cruised through the ham-burg-er stand _
2., 3. *See additional lyrics*

_ now. _   Seems she for - got all a - bout _ the li -

brar - y like she told her "old man" _ now. _   And with her

To Coda ✛

ra - di - o blast - in', goes cruis - in' just as fast as she can _ now. _

Chorus

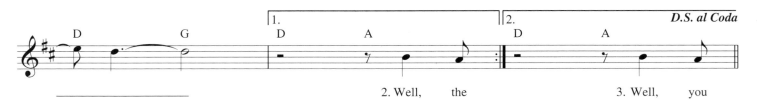

And she'll have fun, fun, fun, till her dad - dy takes the T - bird a - way. _

And she'll have fun, fun, fun, till her dad - dy takes the T - bird a - way. _   2. Well, the   3. Well, you

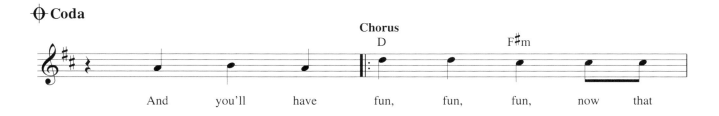

⊕ Coda

Chorus

And you'll have fun, fun, fun, now that

dad - dy took the T - Bird a - way._____

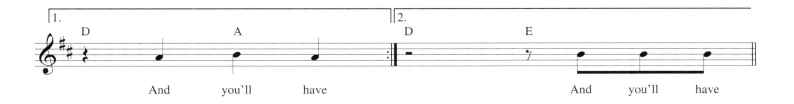

1.

And you'll have

2.

And you'll have

Outro

Repeat and fade

{ fun, } / { Fun, } fun, fun, now that dad - dy took the T - Bird a - way._____

Additional Lyrics

2. Well, the girls can't stand her 'cause she walks, looks and drives like an ace, now.
   She makes the "Indy" Five Hundred look like a Roman chariot race, now.
   A lot of guys try to catch her, but she leads 'em on a wild goose chase, now.

3. Well, you knew all along that your dad was getting wise to you, now.
   And since he took your set of keys, you've been thinking that your fun is all through, now.
   But you can come along with me, 'cause we got a lot of things to do, now.

Great Balls of Fire

Words and Music by Otis Blackwell and Jack Hammer

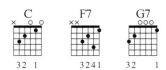

Strum Pattern: 6, 2
Pick Pattern: 4, 2

Verse

Bright Rock

1. You shake my nerves and you rat - tle my brain. __ Too much love drives a

man in - sane. __ You broke my will, but what a thrill. Good - ness gra - cious, great __

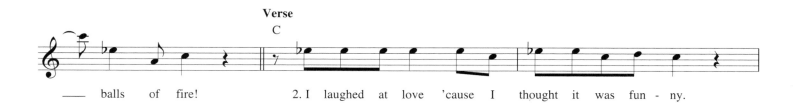

__ balls of fire! 2. I laughed at love 'cause I thought it was fun - ny.

You came a - long and you moved __ me, hon - ey. I changed my mind,

love's just fine. __ Good - ness gra - cious, great __ balls of fire! Kiss me, ba - by.

Woo, __ it feels good. Hold me, ba - by.

Well, I want to love you like a lov-er should.__ You're fine, __

so kind, __ got to tell this world that you're mine, mine, mine, mine.__

Verse

3., 4. I chew my nails and I twid-dle my thumb.__ I'm real ner-vous but it

To Coda ⊕

sure is fun.__ Come on, ba-by, you're driv-ing me cra-zy.

Piano Solo

Good-ness gra-cious, great___ balls of fire!

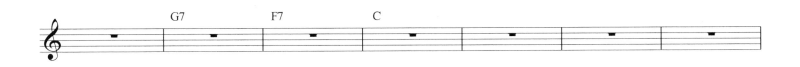

D.S. al Coda

Well,_____

⊕ **Coda**

Good-ness gra-cious, great_____ balls of fire!

The Great Pretender

Words and Music by Buck Ram

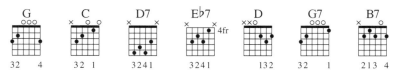

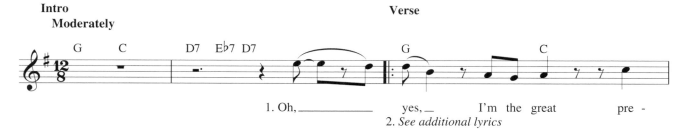

Strum Pattern: 7, 8
Pick Pattern: 7, 8

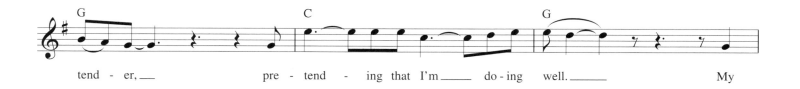

1. Oh, _____ yes, __ I'm the great pre -
2. *See additional lyrics*

tend - er, __ pre - tend - ing that I'm ___ do - ing well. ___ My

need is such I pre - tend ___ too much. I'm lone - ly __ but no one can

tell. _____ 2. Oh, _____ lone. _____ Too real is this feel - ing of

make - be - lieve, too real ___ when I feel what my heart can't con - ceal. 3., 4. Oh, ___

_____ yes, I'm the great pre - tend - er. __ Just

laugh - in' and gay like a clown.____ I seem to be, but I'm / what I'm

G C G D To Coda ⊕ B7

not you see. / I'm wear - ing my heart like a crown; pre - tend -
not you see.

G D G G7 *D.S. al Coda* ⊕ **Coda** B7

- ing____ that you're____ still a - round.____ Too crown; pre -

Freely
N.C. *grad. rit.* C G

tend - ing ____ that you're ____ still a - round.____

Additional Lyrics

2. Oh, yes, I'm the great pretender,
   Adrift in a world of my own;
   I play the game but, to my real shame,
   You've left me to dream all alone.

Guitar Boogie Shuffle

By Arthur Smith

Strum Pattern: 2, 3
Pick Pattern: 3, 4

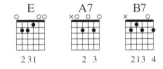

A **Moderate fast Rock**

B

Heartbreak Hotel

Words and Music by Mae Boren Axton, Tommy Durden and Elvis Presley

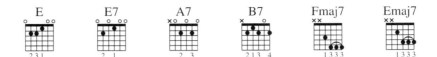

Strum Pattern: 1, 3
Pick Pattern: 3, 5

Verse

Moderate Blues

1. Well, since my ___ ba-by left me, well, I found a new place to dwell. Well, it's
2., 3., 4., 6. *See additional lyrics*
5. *Instrumental*
*N.C. 1st & 2nd times

down at the end of lone-ly street at Heart-break Ho-tel. Well, I'll be, I'll be so lone-ly, ba-by.

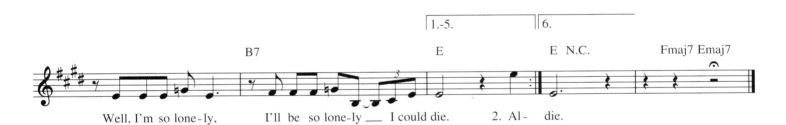

Well, I'm so lone-ly, I'll be so lone-ly ___ I could die. 2. Al- die.

Additional Lyrics

2., 6. Although it's always crowded, you still can find some room
For a broken hearted lovers to cry there in the gloom, and be so...
They'll make you so lonely baby. They'll make you so lonely.
They'll be so lonely they could die.

3. Now the bellhop's tears keep flowing, the desk clerk's dressed in black,
Well, they've been so long on lonely street they'll never, never gonna look back and they're so...
They'll be so lonely baby. Well, they're so lonely.
Well they're so lonely they could die.

4. Well, now if your baby leaves ya and you got a tale to tell,
Well, just take a walk down lonely street to Heartbreak Hotel where you will be...
You'll be so lonely baby; where you will be lonely.
You'll be so lonely you could die.

Heatwave
(Love Is Like a Heatwave)

Words and Music by Edward Holland, Lamont Dozier and Brian Holland

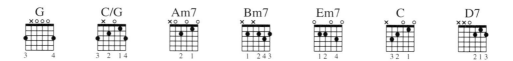

Strum Pattern: 4, 6
Pick Pattern: 1, 3

Intro
Moderately fast

1. When-ev - er I'm

Verse

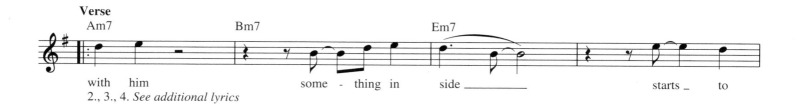

with him _____ some - thing in side _____ starts _ to
2., 3., 4. *See additional lyrics*

burn - in' ___ and ___ I'm filled with _ de - sire. _____

Could it be a dev - il in me ___ or is this the way _ love's sup-posed to be? ___ It's like a

Chorus

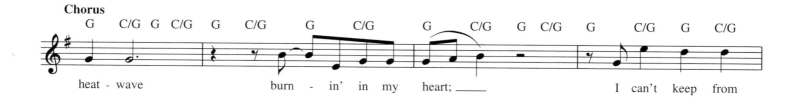

heat - wave burn - in' in my heart; _____ I can't keep from

cry - in'. It's tear - in' me a - part. 2. When - ev - er he

G N.C. Am7 Bm7 Em7

Additional lyrics

2. Whenever he calls my name,
   Soft, low, sweet and plain,
   I feel, yeah, yeah, well,
   I feel that burnin' flame.
   Has high blood pressure got a hold on me
   Or is this the way love's supposed to be?

3. Sometimes I stare into space,
   Tears all over my face;
   I can't explain it, don't understand it,
   I ain't never felt like this before.
   Now that funny feelin' has me amazed;
   I don't know what to do, my head's in a haze.

4. Yeah, yeah, yeah, yeah, yeah.
   Yeah, whoa, ho.
   Yeah, yeah, yeah, yeah, ho.
   Don't pass up this chance,
   This time it's a true romance.

I Want You, I Need You, I Love You

Words by Maurice Mysels
Music by Ira Kosloff

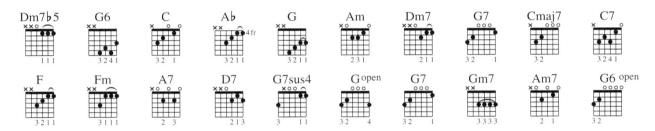

Strum Pattern: 1, 2
Pick Pattern: 2, 4

1. Ho, ho, hold me close, ___ hold me tight; ___ make me

thrill ___ with de - light. ___ Let me know ___ where I stand ___ from the start. ___ I

want you, I need you. ___ I, I love you ___ with all my ___

Hi-Heel Sneakers

Words and Music by Robert Higgenbotham

Strum Pattern: 3, 4
Pick Pattern: 3, 4

red dress, ba - by,   'cause __ we're go - in' out __ to -

2., 4. *See additional lyrics*
3., 5. *Instrumental*

night.   Put on __ your red dress, ba - by,

'cause __ we're go - in' out to - night. __

Bet - ter wear some box - ing gloves, __   in case some

1., 2., 3.   **4. *D.S. and fade***

fool might wan - na fight. __   2., 4. Put on __ your

1. Put on __ your

Additional Lyrics

2. Put on your hi-heel sneakers,
   Wear your wig hat on your head.
   Put on your hi-heel sneakers,
   Wear your wig hat on your head.
   I'm pretty sure now baby,
   'Cause don't you know you're gonna knock 'em dead.

4. Put on your hi-heel sneakers,
   Wear your wig hat on your head.
   Put on your hi-heel sneakers,
   Wear your wig hat on your head.
   I know you realize
   I'm pretty sure you're gonna knock 'em dead.

Hello Mary Lou

Words and Music by Gene Pitney and C. Mangiaracina

Strum Pattern: 4
Pick Pattern: 3

Intro
Moderately

I'm not one that gets a - round, ___ swear my feet stuck to the ground, ___ and

To Coda 2 ⊕

D.S. al Coda 1

though I nev - er did ___ meet you be - fore. ___ I said hel - lo, ___

⊕ **Coda 1**

Guitar Solo

D.S.S. al Coda 2

2. I

⊕ **Coda 2**   *D.S. al Coda 3*   ⊕ **Coda 3**

Hey, hey, hel - lo, ___   So, hel - lo, ___ Mar - y Lou, ___ good - bye

heart.   Yes, hel - lo, Mar - y Lou, ___ good - bye heart.

Additional Lyrics

2. I saw your lips, I heard your voice.
Believe me I just had no choice.
Wild horses couldn't make me stay away.
I thought about a moonlit night,
My arms around you good and tight.
That's all I had to see for me to say...

Hound Dog

Words and Music by Jerry Leiber and Mike Stoller

Strum Pattern: 1
Pick Pattern: 2

I Can't Stop Loving You

Words and Music by Don Gibson

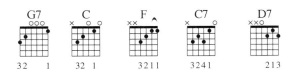

Strum Pattern: 4
Pick Pattern: 3

Additional Lyrics

Chorus I can't stop loving you, there's no use to try.
Pretend there's someone new; I can't live a lie.
I can't stop wanting you the way that I do.
There's only been one love for me, that one love is you.

I Get Around

Words and Music by Brian Wilson and Mike Love

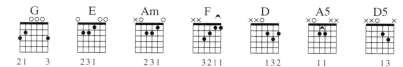

Strum Pattern: 2
Pick Pattern: 4

Intro
Moderately

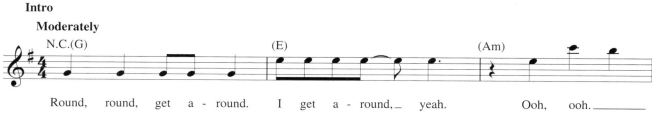

Round, round, get a-round. I get a-round,___ yeah. Ooh, ooh._____
(Get a-round, round, round,

Chorus

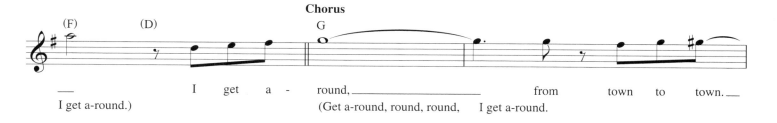

___ I get a-round,_____ from town to town.___
I get a-round.) (Get a-round, round, round, I get a-round.

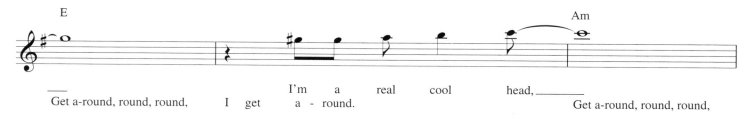

___ Get a-round, round, round, I get a-round. I'm a real cool head,_____
Get a-round, round, round,

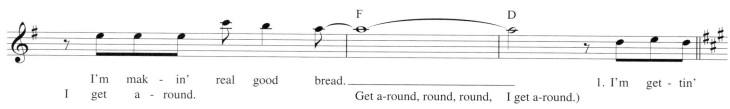

I'm mak-in' real good bread._____ 1. I'm get-tin'
I get a-round. Get a-round, round, round, I get a-round.)

Verse

bugged driv-in' up and down the same old strip. I got-ta find a new place where the
2. *See additional lyrics*

kids are hip. My

bud - dies and me___ are get - tin' real well known.___ Yeah, the bad guys know us and they

% Chorus

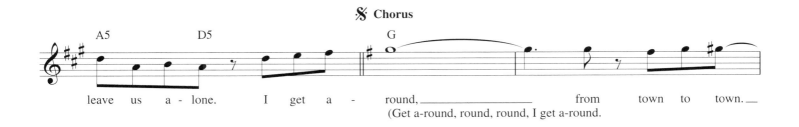

leave us a - lone. I get a - round,_____ from town to town.___
(Get a-round, round, round, I get a-round.

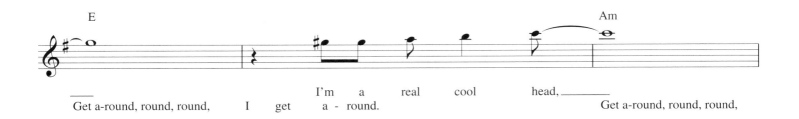

Get a-round, round, round, I get a - round. I'm a real cool head,_____ Get a-round, round, round,

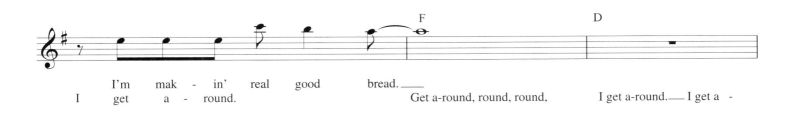

I'm mak - in' real good bread.___ I get a - round. Get a-round, round, round, I get a-round.___ I get a -

round._____ Get a-round, round, round.) 2. We round.)___ I get a -

Additional Lyrics

2. We always take my car 'cause it's never been beat.
And we've never missed yet with the girls we meet.
None of the guys go steady 'cause it wouldn't be right
To leave their best girl home on a Saturday night.

I Love How You Love Me

Words and Music by Barry Mann and Larry Kolber

Additional Lyrics

2., 4. I love how your heart beats whenever I hold you.
I love how you think of me without being told to.
And I love the way your touch is almost heavenly;
But darling most of all, I love how you love me.

I'm Leaving It Up To You

Words and Music by Don Harris and Dewey Terry, Jr.

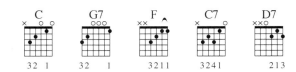

Strum Pattern: 1
Pick Pattern: 4

1. I'm leav-in' it all up to (2., 3.) you.____ You de-cide____

what you're gon-na do. Now do you want my love,____ or are we

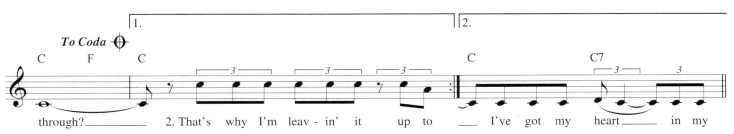

through?____ 2. That's why I'm leav-in' it up to ____ I've got my heart____ in my

Bridge

hand.____ I, I, I don't un-der-stand,____ what have I done

D.S. al Coda

wrong?____ I wor-ship the ground____ you walk on. 3. That's why I'm leav-in' it up to

Coda

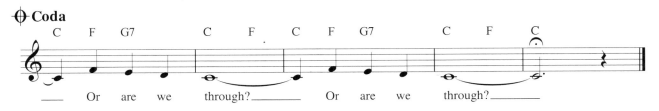

____ Or are we through?____ Or are we through?____

It's My Party

Words and Music by Herb Wiener, Wally Gold and John Gluck, Jr.

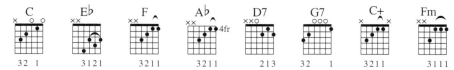

Strum Pattern: 3, 6
Pick Pattern: 4, 5

Verse
Moderately bright

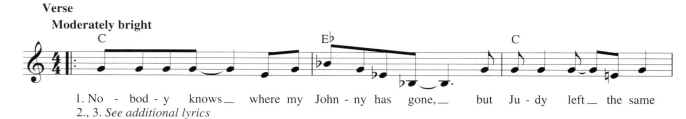

1. No - bod - y knows___ where my John - ny has gone,___ but Ju - dy left___ the same
2., 3. *See additional lyrics*

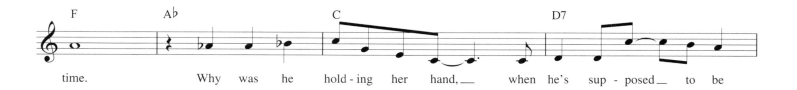

time. Why was he hold - ing her hand,___ when he's sup - posed___ to be

Chorus

mine?_____ It's my par - ty, and I'll cry if I want___ to,

cry if I want___ to, cry if I want___ to. You would cry

too if it hap - pened to you.

Additional Lyrics

2. Play all my records; keep dancing all night,
   But leave alone for awhile.
   'Til Johnny's dancing with me,
   I've got no reason to smile.

3. Judy and Johnny just walked through the door,
   Like a queen with her king.
   Oh, what a birthday surprise,
   Judy's wearing his ring.

It's Only Make Believe

Words and Music by Conway Twitty and Jack Nance

Additional lyrics

2. My hopes, my dreams come true,
My life I'd give for you,
My heart, a wedding ring,
My all my everything.
My heart I can't control,
You rule my very soul,
My only prayer will be
Someday you'll care for me
But it's only make believe.

Jailhouse Rock

Words and Music by Jerry Leiber and Mike Stoller

Strum Pattern: 2
Pick Pattern: 4

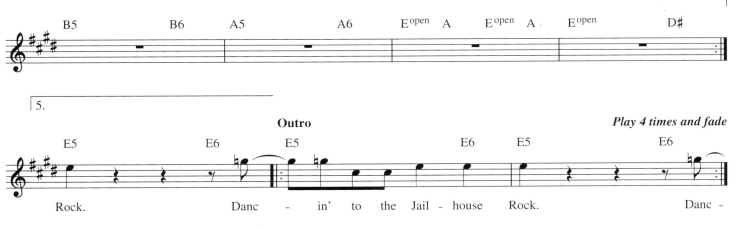

|5.|

Outro

Play 4 times and fade

Rock.   Danc - in' to the Jail - house Rock.   Danc -

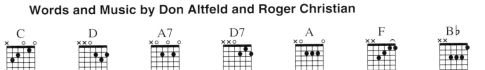

Additional Lyrics

2. Spider Murphy played the tenor saxophone.
   Little Joe was blowin' on the slide trombone.
   The drummer boy from Illinois went crash, boom, bang.
   The whole rhythm section was the Purple Gang.

3. Number forty-seven said to number three,
   "You the cutest jailbird I ever did see.
   I sure would be delighted with your company.
   Come on, and do the Jailhouse Rock with me."

4. Sad Sack was sittin' on a block of stone,
   Way over in the corner weepin' all alone.
   The warden said, "Hey, buddy, don't you be no square.
   If you can't find a partner use a wooden chair."

5. Shifty Henry said to Bugs, "For heaven's sake,
   No one's lookin', now's our chance to make a break."
   Bugs, he turned to Shifty and he said, "Nix, nix,
   I wanna stick around awhile and get my kicks."

The Little Old Lady (From Pasadena)

Words and Music by Don Altfeld and Roger Christian

Strum Pattern: 1, 3
Pick Pattern: 3, 5

Verse

Moderately

G

1. The lit - tle old la - dy from Pas - a - de - na
2., 3. *See additional lyrics*

(Go gran-ny, go, gran-ny,

C   G

has a pret - ty lit - tle flow - er bed of white gar - de - nias.

go, gran-ny, go.) —

But parked in a rick - et - y

(Go, gran-ny, go, gran-ny, go, gran-ny, go.) —

old ga - age, __ there's a brand new shin - y sup - er - stocked Dodge. _____

Chorus

— And ev - 'ry - bod - y's say - in' that there's no - bod - y mean - er than the

lit - tle old la - dy from Pas - a - de - na. She drives real fast and she

drives real hard. __ She's the ter - ror of Col - o - ra - do Boul - e - vard. __ It's the

1., 2.

lit - tle old la - dy from Pas - a - de - na! 2. If you

3. **Chorus** *Repeat and fade*

The lit - tle old la - dy from Pas - a - de - na. The

Additional Lyrics

2. If you see her on the strip don't try to choose her.
   You might have goer, but you'll never lose her.
   She's gonna get a ticket now, sooner or later,
   'Cause she can't keep her foot off the accelerator.

3. You'll see her all the time just gettin' her kicks now,
   With a four-speed stick and a four-two-six now.
   The guys come to race her from miles around,
   But she'll give 'em a length, then she'll shut 'em down.

Let's Twist Again

Words by Kal Mann
Music by Dave Appell and Kal Mann

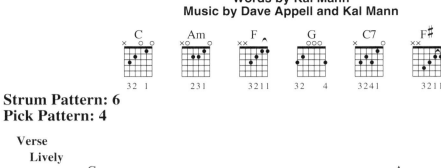

Strum Pattern: 6
Pick Pattern: 4

Verse
Lively

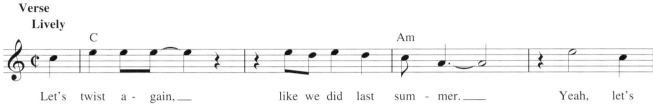

Let's twist a - gain, ___ like we did last sum - mer. ___ Yeah, let's

twist a - gain, ___ like we did last year. ___ Don't - cha re - mem - ber when

things were real - ly hum - min'? ___ Yeah, let's twist a - gain, ___ twist-in' time is here. ___

Bridge

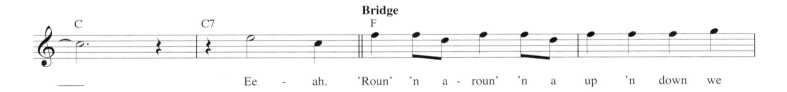

___ Ee - ah. 'Roun' 'n a - roun' 'n a up 'n down we

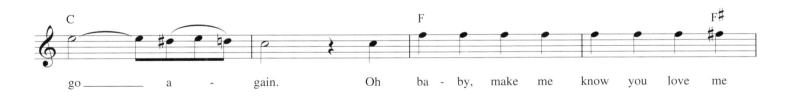

go ___ a - gain. Oh ba - by, make me know you love me

Outro

so, ___ an' ___ then... Let's twist a - gain, ___ like we did last sum - mer. ___

Yeah, let's twist a - gain, ___ like we did last year. ___

Kansas City

Words and Music by Jerry Leiber and Mike Stoller

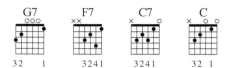

Strum Pattern: 2, 3
Pick Pattern: 3, 4

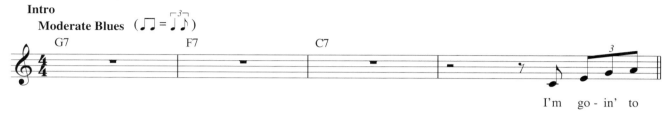

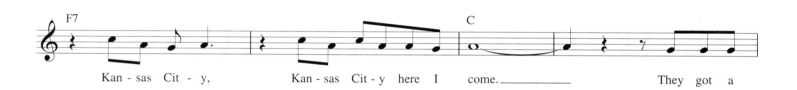

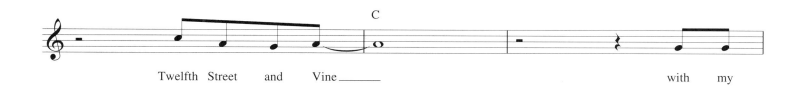

Twelfth Street and Vine _____ with my

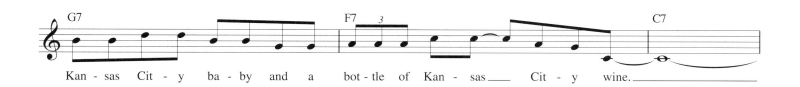

Kan - sas Cit - y ba - by and a bot - tle of Kan - sas ___ Cit - y wine. _____

Bridge

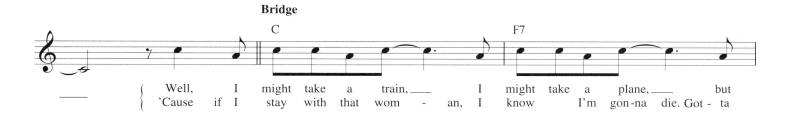

{ Well, I might take a train, ___ I might take a plane, ___ but

'Cause if I stay with that wom - an, I know I'm gon-na die. Got - ta

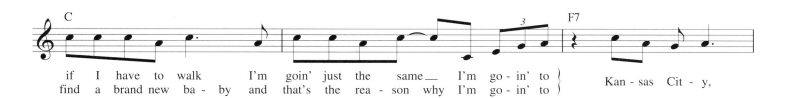

if I have to walk I'm goin' just the same ___ I'm go - in' to }

find a brand new ba - by and that's the rea - son why I'm go - in' to } Kan - sas Cit - y,

Kan - sas Cit - y here I come. _____ They got a cra - zy way of lov - in' there and

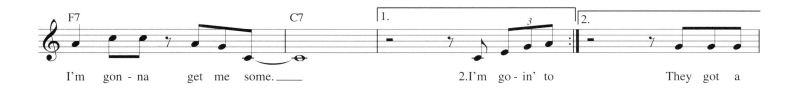

I'm gon - na get me some. ___ 2.I'm go - in' to They got a

cra - zy way of lov - in' there and I'm gon - na get me some. _____

Additional Lyrics

2. I'm goin' to pack my clothes, leave at the crack of dawn.
   I'm goin' to pack my clothes, leave at the crack of dawn.
   My old lady will be sleepin' and she won't know where I've gone.

La Bamba

By Ritchie Valens

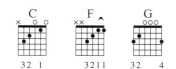

Strum Pattern: 2, 3
Pick Pattern: 3, 4

Intro %

Moderate Latin Rock

G A B C E D F A G G B C A B D
G

Verse

1., 4. Pa - ra bai - lar la bam - ba. Pa - ra bai - lar la bam-

- ba se ne - ce - si - ta un - a po - ca de gra - cia.

to need   little   grace
              not much   good

Un - a po - ca de gra - cia pa ra mi pa ra ti ____ y ar - ri - ba ar - ri -

- ba; ar - ri - ba ar - ri - ba por ti se re ____

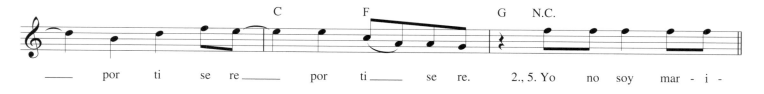

____ por ti se re ____ por ti se re. 2., 5. Yo no soy mar - i -

Limbo Rock

Words and Music by Billy Strange and Jon Sheldon

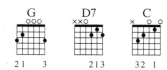

Strum Pattern: 4, 3
Pick Pattern: 6, 3

Intro
Moderate Latin Rock

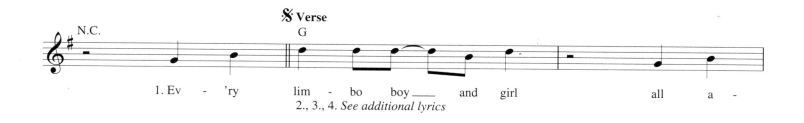

1. Ev - 'ry lim - bo boy___ and girl all a -
2., 3., 4. *See additional lyrics*

round the lim - bo world, gon - na do the Lim - bo Rock

all a - round the lim - bo clock. Jack be

Chorus

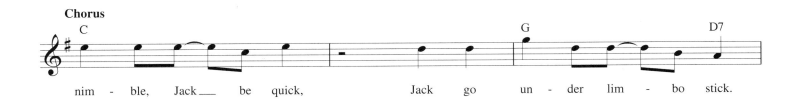

nim - ble, Jack __ be quick, Jack go un - der lim - bo stick.

To Coda 1 ⊕

To Coda 2 ⊕

Fine

All a - round the lim - bo clock, hey, let's do the Lim - bo Rock.

Breakdown

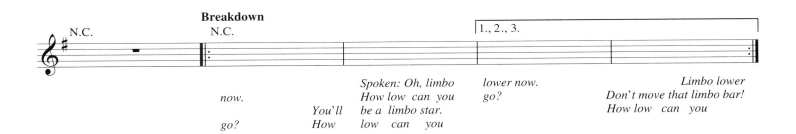

Spoken: Oh, limbo lower now.
How low can you go?
now.
You'll be a limbo star.
Limbo lower
Don't move that limbo bar!
How low can you
go?
How low can you

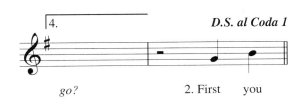
D.S. al Coda 1

go? 2. First you

⊕ **Coda 1**

D.S. al Coda 2

3. La, la

⊕ **Coda 2**
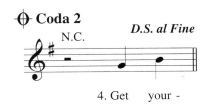
D.S. al Fine

4. Get your -

Additional lyrics

2. First you spread your limbo feet,
   Then you move to limbo beat.
   Limbo ankle, limbo knee;
   Bend back, like the limbo tree.

3. La, la, la, la, la, la, la... etc.
   (cont. through Chorus)

4. Get yourself a limbo girl,
   Give that chick a limbo whirl.
   There's a limbo moon above,
   You will fall in limbo love.

Little Deuce Coupe

Music by Brian Wilson
Words by Roger Christian

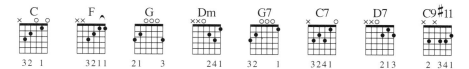

Strum Pattern: 2, 3
Pick Pattern: 3, 4

Verse
Moderate Rock

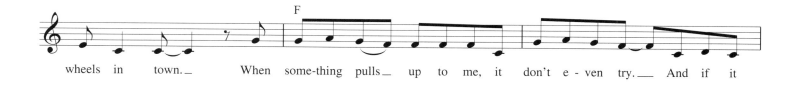

1. Well, I'm not brag- gin', babe, so don't put me down, ___ but I've got the fast - est set of
2. *See additional lyrics*

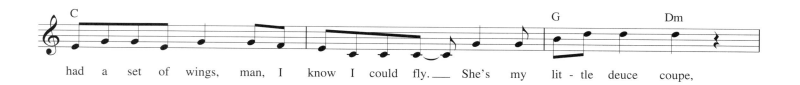

wheels in town. ___ When some-thing pulls ___ up to me, it don't e - ven try. ___ And if it

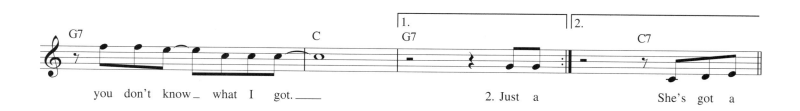

had a set of wings, man, I know I could fly. ___ She's my lit - tle deuce coupe,

you don't know ___ what I got. ___   2. Just a   She's got a

Bridge

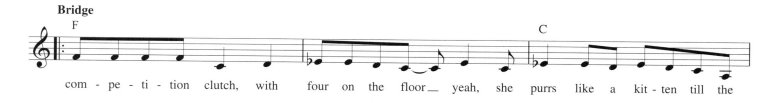

com - pe - ti - tion clutch, with four on the floor ___ yeah, she purrs like a kit - ten till the

lake pipes roar. ___ And if that ain't e-nough to make you flip your wig, ___ there's

Outro

one more thing, I've got the pink slip, dad-dy! And com-in' off the line, when the

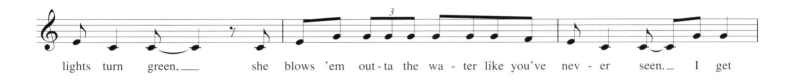

lights turn green, ___ she blows 'em out-ta the wa-ter like you've nev-er seen. ___ I get

pushed out of shape, ___ and it's hard to steer, ___ when I get rub-ber in a

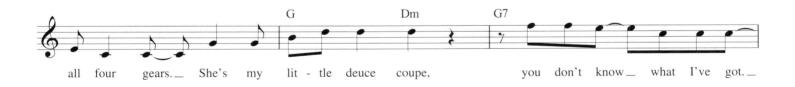

all four gears. ___ She's my lit-tle deuce coupe, you don't know ___ what I've got. ___

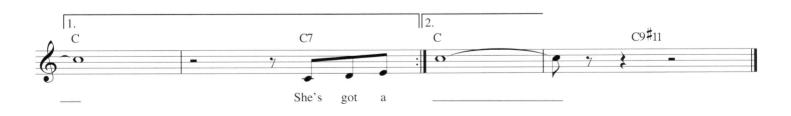

She's got a ___

Additional Lyrics

2. Just a little deuce coupe with a flathead mill,
   But she'll walk a Thunderbird like it's standin' still.
   She's ported and relieved, and she's stroked and she's bored.
   She'll do a hundred and forty with the top end floored.
   She's my little deuce coupe,
   You don't know what I got.

The Loco-Motion

Words and Music by Gerry Goffin and Carole King

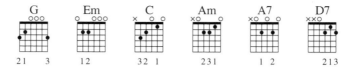

Strum Pattern: 3, 4
Pick Pattern: 6

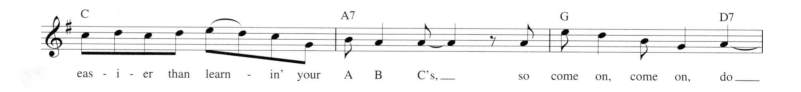

D7

___ Oh, well, I think you got the knack.

Verse

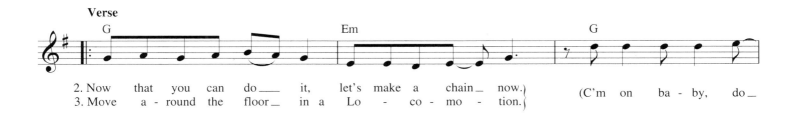

G   Em   G

2. Now that you can do___ it, let's make a chain___ now.)   (C'm on ba - by, do___
3. Move a - round the floor___ in a Lo - co - mo - tion.)

Em   G   Em

___ the Lo - co - mo - tion.) A chug - a - chug - a mo - tion like a rail - road train___ now.)
         Do it hold - in' hands___ if___ you get the no - tion.)

G   Em   C

(C'm on ba - by, do___ the Lo - co - mo - tion.) Do it nice and eas - y now,___
         There's nev - er been a dance___ that's so

Am   C   A7

don't lose con - trol.___ A lit - tle bit of rhy - thm and a lot of soul.___
eas - y to do.___ It'll e - ven make you hap - py when you're feel - in' blue.___ So,

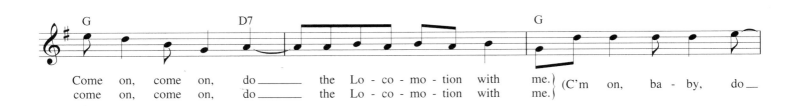

G   D7   G

Come on, come on, do___ the Lo - co - mo - tion with me.) (C'm on, ba - by, do___
come on, come on, do___ the Lo - co - mo - tion with me.)

Outro   *Repeat and fade*

Em   G   Em

___ the Lo - co - mo - tion.) (C'm on, ba - by, do___ the Lo - co - mo - tion.)

Long Tall Sally

Words and Music by Enotris Johnson, Richard Penniman and Robert Blackwell

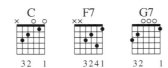

Strum pattern: 2, 3
Pick Pattern: 2, 3

1. Gon - na tell Aunt Mar - y a - bout Un - cle John. He claims he has the mis - 'ry, but he
2., 3., 4. *See additional lyrics*

has a lot of fun. Oh, ba - by, yes, _____ ba - by.

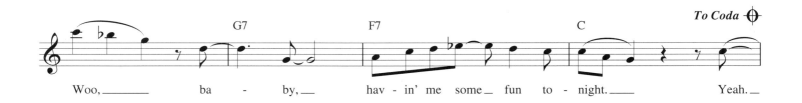

Woo, _____ ba - by, _____ hav - in' me some ___ fun to - night. _____ Yeah. ___

_____ 2. Well, ___ Ow! ___

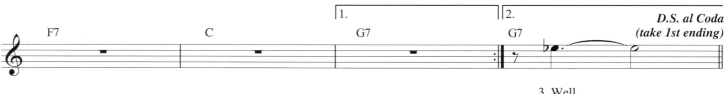

3. Well, _____

We're gon-na have some fun to-night.___ We're gon-na have some fun to-night.___

___ Ooh,___ have some fun___ to - night.___ Ev - 'ry - thing's al -

right.___ Have some fun, have me some fun to - night.___

Additional Lyrics

2., 4. Well, long tall Sally, she's built pretty sweet.
She's got ev'rything that Uncle John need.
Oh, baby, yes, baby.
Woo, baby, havin' me some fun tonight. Yeah.

3. Well, I saw Uncle John with blonde headed Sally.
He saw Aunt Mary comin' and he ducked back in the alley.
Oh, baby, yes, baby.
Woo, baby, havin' me some fun tonight. Yeah. Ow!

Love Potion Number 9

Words and Music by Jerry Leiber and Mike Stoller

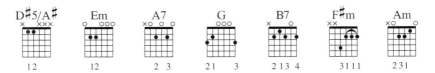

Strum Pattern: 1
Pick Pattern: 1

% **Verse**
Moderately bright

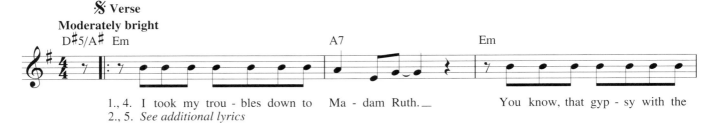

1., 4. I took my trou - bles down to Ma - dam Ruth.___ You know, that gyp - sy with the
2., 5. See additional lyrics

gold - capped tooth.___ She's got a pad down at Thir - ty - fourth and Vine,

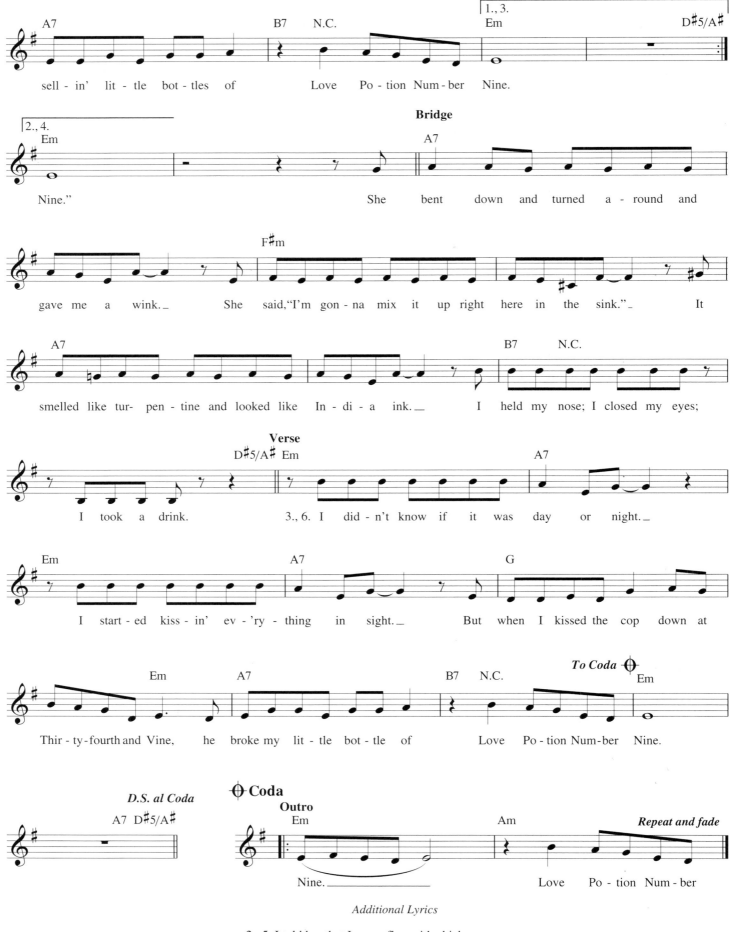

Additional Lyrics

2., 5. I told her that I was a flop with chicks.
I've been this way since nineteen fifty-six.
She looked at my palm and she made a magic sign.
She said, "What you need is Love Potion Number Nine."

Louie, Louie

Words and Music by Richard Berry

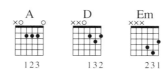

Strum Pattern: 3, 5
Pick Pattern: 3, 4

* Lyrics omitted at the request of the publisher.

Love Me Tender

Words and Music by Elvis Presley and Vera Matson

Strum Pattern: 4
Pick Pattern: 6

Verse
Slowly

1. Love me ten - der, love me sweet, nev - er let me go. You have made my
2. *See additional lyrics*

Chorus

life com - plete, and I love you so. Love me ten - der, love me true,

all my dreams ful - fill. For, my dar - lin', I love you, and I al - ways will.

Verse

3. Love me ten - der, love me dear, tell me you are mine. I'll be yours through

Outro-Chorus

all the years, till the end of time. Love me ten - der, love me true,

all my dreams ful - fill. For, my dar - lin', I love you, and I al - ways will.

Additional Lyrics

2. Love me tender, love me long,
   Take me to your heart.
   For it's there that I belong,
   And we'll never part.

Money
(That's What I Want)

Words and Music by Berry Gordy and Janie Bradford

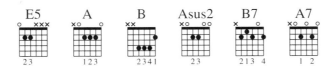

Strum Pattern: 2
Pick Pattern: 4

Intro
Moderate Rock

Verse

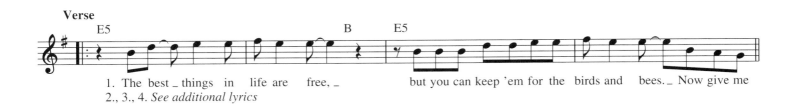

1. The best _ things in life are free, _ but you can keep 'em for the birds and bees. _ Now give me
2., 3., 4. *See additional lyrics*

Chorus

mon - ey, that's what I want,
(That's what I want.) _
that's what I
(That's what I want.) _

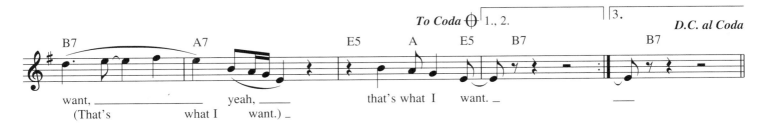

To Coda ⊕ |1., 2.| |3.| *D.C. al Coda*

want, _____ yeah, _____ that's what I want. _
(That's what I want.) _

⊕ Coda

Verse

5., 6. Well, __ now give me mon-ey, _____ a lot-ta mon-ey, (That's
(That's what I want.) _ (That's

I wan - na be free. _ Oh, _____ lot - ta mon - ey.
You need mon - ey. _____ Oh, now, gim - me mon - ey.
what I want.) _ (That's what I want.) _ (That's

That's what I want, _____ yeah, _____ that's what I want. __
what I want.) _ (That's what I want.) _

Additional Lyrics

2. Your lovin' give me a thrill,
   But your lovin' don't pay my bills.

3., 4. Money don't get ev'rything it's true,
   What it don't get I can't use.

Nadine

(Is It You)
Words and Music by Chuck Berry

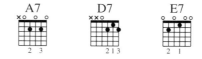

Strum Pattern: 2, 4
Pick Pattern: 3, 4

Intro
Moderate fast Rock

1. As

Verse

I got on a cit - y bus and found a va - cant seat, I thought I saw my fu - ture bride _
2., 3., 4. *See additional lyrics*

walk - in' down the street. I shout - ed to the driv - er, "Hey con - duc - tor, you must _ slow down, _

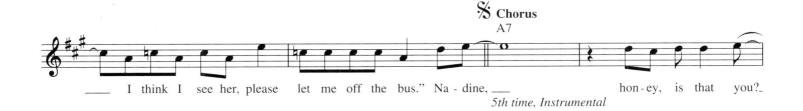

%. **Chorus**

_____ I think I see her, please let me off the bus." Na-dine, ___ hon-ey, is that you?_

5th time, Instrumental

_____ Oh, __ Na - dine, _____ hon-ey, {is that / where are / is that / is that} you?_

_____ Seem like ev - 'ry time I {see you, dar-lin', / catch up wid-ya, / catch up wid-ya, / see you, dar-lin',}

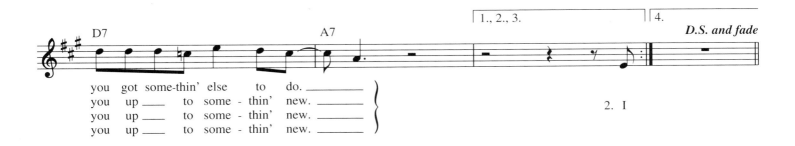

1., 2., 3.   4.

D.S. and fade

you got some-thin' else to do. _____
you up ___ to some - thin' new. _____
you up ___ to some - thin' new. _____
you up ___ to some - thin' new. _____

2. I

Additional Lyrics

2. I saw her from the corner when she turned and doubled back,
   She started walkin' toward a coffee colored Cadillac.
   I's pushin' through the crowd, try'n' to get where she was at
   And I was campaign shoutin' like a southern diplomat.

3. Downtown searching for her, looking all around.
   Saw her getting in a yellow cab, heading uptown.
   I caught a loaded taxi, paid up everybody's tab.
   Flipped a twenty dollar bill and told them, "Catch that yellow cab."

4. She moves around like a wayward summer breeze.
   Go, driver. Go, catch her for me please.
   Moving through the traffic like a mounted cavalier.
   Leaning out the taxi window trying to make her hear.

My Boyfriend's Back

Words and Music by Robert Feldman, Gerald Goldstein and Richard Gottehrer

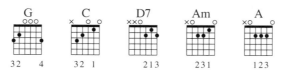

Strum Pattern: 3, 4
Pick Pattern: 3, 4

Verse
Moderately fast

1. My boy-friend's back, and you're gon-na be in trou-ble.
2. *See additional lyrics*

(Hey, la - di -

When you see him com - in', bet - ter cut on the dou - ble.
la, my boy-friend's back.

Hey, la - di - la, my boy-friend's back.

You've been spread - in' lies that

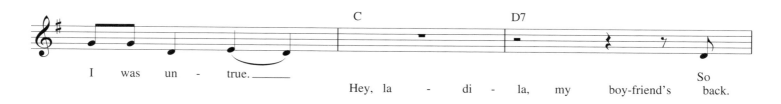

I was un - true. ___

Hey, la - di - la, my boy-friend's back.

So

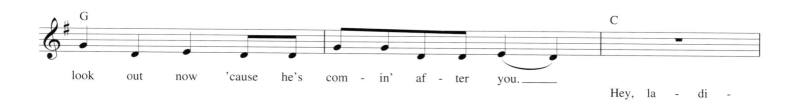

look out now 'cause he's com - in' af - ter you. ___

Hey, la - di -

la, my boy-friend's back.)

And ___ he knows that you've been try - in',

Additional Lyrics

2. He's been gone for such a long time.
Now he's back and things will be fine.
You're gonna be sorry you were ever born,
'Cause he's kind of big and he's awful strong.
And he know's about your cheatin',
Now you're gonna get a beatin'.

No Particular Place to Go

Words and Music by Chuck Berry

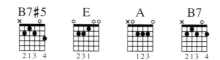

Strum Pattern: 1
Pick Pattern: 2

1. Rid-ing a-long in my au-to-mo-bile,

2., 3., 4. See additional lyrics

my ba-by be-side me at the wheel. I stole a kiss at the turn of a

mile, my cu-ri-os-i-ty run-ning wild.

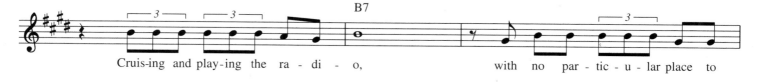

Cruis-ing and play-ing the ra-di-o, with no par-tic-u-lar place to

1., 2., 3. go. 2. Rid-ing a-long in my au-to-mo- **4.** go.

Additional Lyrics

2. Riding along in my automobile,
   I was anxious to tell her the way I feel.
   So I told her softly and sincere
   And she leaned and whispered in my ear.
   Cuddling more and driving slow,
   With no particular place to go.

3. No particular place to go,
   So we parked way out on the cocamo.
   The night was young and the moon was gold,
   So we both decided to take a stroll.
   Can you imagine the way I felt?
   I couldn't unfasten her safety belt.

4. Riding along in my calaboose,
   Still trying to get her belt unloose.
   All the way home I held a grudge,
   For the safety belt that wouldn't budge.
   Cruising and playing the radio,
   With no particular place to go.

Not Fade Away

Words and Music by Charles Hardin and Norman Petty

Strum Pattern: 2
Pick Pattern: 4

Additional Lyrics

2. My love is bigger than a Cadillac.
   I try to show it and you drive me back.
   Your love for me got to be real,
   For you to know-a just how I feel.
   A love for real'll not fade away.

3. I'm a-gonna tell you how it's gonna be.
   You're gonna give-a your love to me.
   A love to last more than one day.
   A love that's love'll not fade away.
   A love that's love'll not fade away.

Oh, Pretty Woman

Words and Music by Roy Orbison and Bill Dees

say you'll stay with me. _____ 'Cause I need you, _____ I'll treat you right.

Come to me ba - by, _____ be mine to - night. _____ 3. Pret - ty

Verse

wom- an, __ don't walk on by; _ pret-ty wom-an, __ don't make me cry; _ pret-ty wom-an, _____

_____ don't walk a - way. _ Hey, _____ O. K. If that's the

way it must be O. K. I guess I'll go on home; it's late. There'll be to -

mor - row night but wait! What do I see? _____

_____ Is she walk - ing back to me? _____ Yeah, she's

walk - ing back to me! _____ Oh, _____ pret - ty wom-an.

Additional Lyrics

2. Pretty woman, won't you pardon me?
Pretty woman, I couldn't help but see;
Pretty woman, that you look lovely as can be.
Are you lonely just like me?

Only the Lonely
(Know the Way I Feel)

Words and Music by Roy Orbison and Joe Melson

* **Strum Pattern: 4**
* **Pick Pattern: 5**

Intro
Moderately

(Dum, dum, dum dum, dig - gy do, wah. ___ Ooh, yay yay,

* Use Pattern 10 for 2/4 measures.

yay, yeah. ___ Oh, oh, oh, oh, ___ ah, _____

___ on - ly the lone - ly. On - ly the lone - ly.) ___

Verse

1. On - ly the lone - ly know the way I ___ feel to -
2. *See additional lyrics*

night. On - ly ___ the lone - ly

know this feel - ing ___ ain't right.

There goes— my ba-by; there goes my heart.

They've gone for-ev-er;_____ so far a-part.

But on-ly the lone-ly know why_____

I cry, on-ly the lone-ly._____
(Dum, dum, dum,

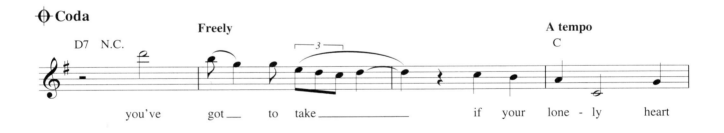

⊕ Coda

you've got— to take_____ if your lone-ly heart

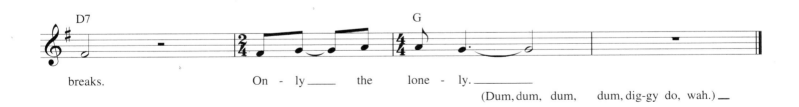

breaks. On-ly— the lone-ly._____
(Dum, dum, dum, dum, dig-gy do, wah.) —

Additional Lyrics

2. Only the lonely know the heartaches I've been through.
Only the lonely know I cry and cry for you.
Maybe tomorrow, a new romance,
No more sorrow, but that's the chance
You've got to take as your lonely heart breaks.
Only the lonely.

Peggy Sue

Words and Music by Jerry Allison, Norman Petty and Buddy Holly

Strum Pattern: 1
Pick Pattern: 2

Additional Lyrics

2. Peggy Sue, Peggy Sue,
   Oh how my heart yearns for you,
   Oh Peggy, my Pa-heggy Sue.
   Oh well, I love you gal, Peggy Sue.

3. I love you, Peggy Sue,
   With a love so rare and true,
   Oh Peggy, my Peggy Sue.
   Oh well, I love you gal, I want you Peggy Sue.

Peppermint Twist

Words and Music by Joseph DiNicola and Henry Glover

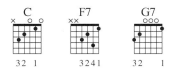

Strum Pattern: 1
Pick Pattern: 2

Verse
Fast Rock

1. Got a new dance and it goes like this.　Name of this dance is the

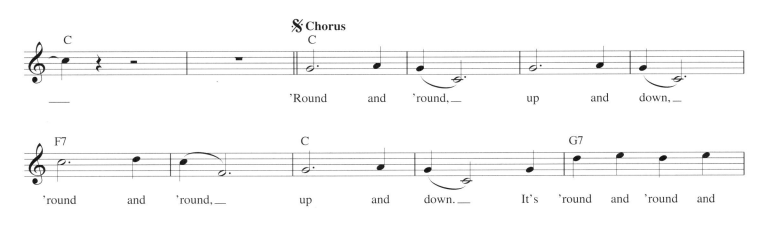

Pep - per - mint Twist.　You'll like _____ it like this, ___ the Pep - per - mint Twist. ___

℠ Chorus

_____ 'Round and 'round, ___ up and down, ___

'round and 'round, ___ up and down. ___ It's 'round and 'round and

Fine **Verse**

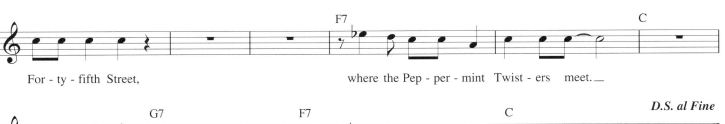

up and down,　one - two - three kick,　one - two - three jump! 2. Meet me, ba - by, on

For - ty - fifth Street,　where the Pep - per - mint Twist - ers meet. ___

D.S. al Fine

You'll learn _____ to do this, ___ the Pep - per - mint Twist. ___

Please Mr. Postman

Words and Music by Robert Bateman, Georgia Dobbins, William Garrett, Freddie Gorman and Brian Holland

Additional Lyrics

2. So many days you've passed me by,
   See the tears standin' in my eyes.
   You didn't stop to make me feel better
   By leaving me a card or a letter.

The Promised Land

Words and Music by Chuck Berry

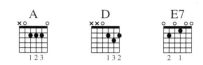

Strum Pattern: 2
Pick Pattern: 4

Verse
Moderately

1. I left my home in Nor-folk, Vir-gin-ia, Cal-i-for-nia on my
2. *See additional lyrics*

mind. _____ I strad-dled that Grey-hound and rode ___ him in-to Ral-eigh and on ___

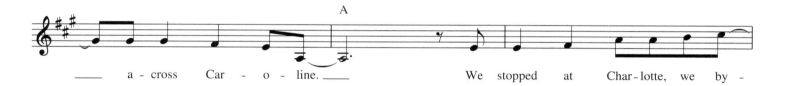

___ a-cross Car-o-line. ___ We stopped at Char-lotte, we by-

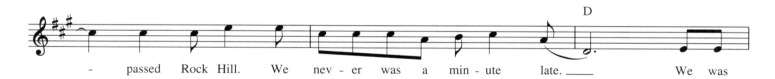

-passed Rock Hill. We nev-er was a min-ute late. ___ We was

nine-ty miles out of At-lan-ta by sun-down, roll-in' out of Geor-gia state. _

___ We had mo-tor trou-ble that turned _____ in-to a strug-gle, half-

way a-cross Al-a-bam'. _____ And that 'Hound broke down and

left   us   all __ strand-ed   in   down-town   Birm - ing - ham. __

Additional Lyrics

2. Right away I bought me a through train ticket,
   Ridin' across Mississippi clean,
   And I was on the Midnight Flyer out of Birmingham,
   Smokin' into New Orleans.
   Somebody helped me get out of Louisiana.
   Just to help me get to Houston Town
   There are people there who care a little about me,
   And they won't let a poor boy down,
   Sure as you're born, they bought me a silk suit,
   They put luggage in my hand,
   And I woke up high over Albuquerque
   On a jet to the Promised Land.

3. Workin' on a T bone steak,
   I had a party flyin' over to the Golden State,
   When the pilot told us in thirteen minutes
   He would get us at the Terminal Gate.
   Swing low, chariot, come down easy,
   Taxi to the Terminal Line;
   Cut your engines, and cool your wings,
   And let me make it to the telephone.
   Los Angeles, give me Norfolk, Virginia.
   Tidewater 4-10-0-0,
   Tell the folks back home this is the Promised Land callin'
   And the poor boy's on the line.

Rockin' Robin

Words and Music by J. Thomas

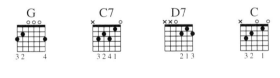

Strum Pattern: 5
Pick Pattern: 1

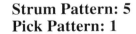

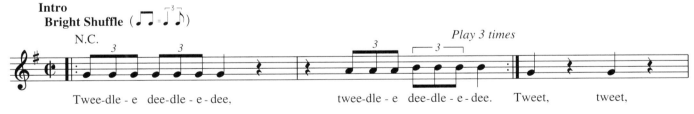

Twee-dle - e dee-dle - e - dee,   twee-dle - e dee-dle - e - dee.   Tweet,   tweet,

tweet,   tweet.   1. He (3.) rocks   in   the   tree - top   all __ the   day   long,   hop -
                        2. *See additional lyrics*

-pin' and a-bop-pin' and a-sing-in' his song. All the lit-tle birds on

Jay - bird Street _ love ___ to hear the rob - in go - in' tweet, tweet, tweet. Rock - in'

Chorus

C7   G

rob - in,   rock, rock, ___ rock - in' rob - in.

D7   C7   G   *To Coda* ⊕ | 1.

Blow, rock - in' rob - in, 'cause we're real - ly gon - na rock to - night. ___

| 2.   **Bridge**

C

A pret - ty lit - tle rav - en at the bird band - stand taught _

G   C

___ him how to do the bop and it was grand. They start - ed go - in' stead - y and

D.S. al Coda

D7   N.C.

bless my soul, he out - bopped the buz - zard and the or - i - ole. 3. He

⊕ **Coda**

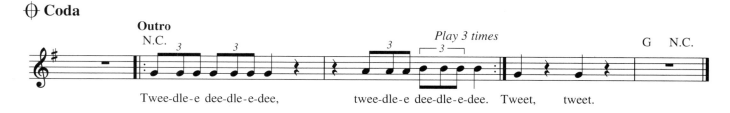

Outro

N.C.   *Play 3 times*   G   N.C.

Twee-dle-e dee-dle-e-dee,   twee-dle-e dee-dle-e-dee. Tweet,   tweet.

Additional Lyrics

2. Ev'ry little swallow, ev'ry chickadee,
   Ev'ry little bird in the tall oak tree.
   The wise old owl, the big black crow,
   Flap their wings singin' go, bird, go.

Rebel 'Rouser

By Duane Eddy and Lee Hazlewood

Red River Rock

Written by Tom King, Ira Mack and Fred Mendelsohn

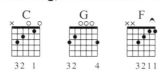

Strum Pattern: 2
Pick Pattern: 4

Moderately bright Rock

D.S. and fade
(take 1st ending)

Rock Around the Clock

Words and Music by Max C. Freedman and Jimmy DeKnight

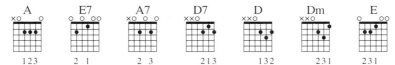

Strum Pattern: 1
Pick Pattern: 2

Intro
Bright Shuffle

One, two, three o' - clock, four o' - clock rock, five, six, sev-en o' - clock, eight o' - clock rock,

nine, ten, e - lev - en o' - clock, twelve o' - clock rock, we're gon - na rock a - round the

Verse

clock to - night.___ 1. Put your glad rags on and join me, hon.___ We'll have some fun when the
2., 4., 5., 6. *See additional lyrics*
3. *Instrumental*

clock strikes one.__ We're gon - na rock a - round the clock to - night, __ we're gon - na rock, rock, rock, 'til

broad day - light.__ We're gon - na rock, gon - na rock a - round__ the clock__ to - night.__

_____ 2. When the ___

Additional Lyrics

2. When the clock strikes two, and three and four,
   If the band slows down we'll yell for more.
   We're gonna rock around the clock tonight,
   We're gonna rock, rock, rock, 'til broad daylight.
   We're gonna rock, gonna rock around the clock tonight.

4. When the chimes ring five and six and seven,
   We'll be rockin' up in seventh heav'n.
   We're gonna rock around the clock tonight,
   We're gonna rock, rock rock, 'til broad daylight.
   We're gonna rock, gonna rock around the clock tonight.

5. When it's eight, nine, ten, eleven, too,
   I'll be goin' strong and so will you.
   We're gonna rock around the clock tonight,
   We're gonna rock, rock, rock, 'til broad daylight.
   We're gonna rock, gonna rock around the clock tonight.

6. When the clock strikes twelve, we'll cool off, then,
   Start a rockin' 'round the clock again.
   We're gonna rock around the clock tonight,
   We're gonna rock, rock, rock, 'til broad daylight.
   We're gonna rock, gonna rock around the clock tonight.

Rock and Roll Is Here to Stay

Words and Music by David White

Strum Pattern: 3
Pick Pattern: 3

Intro
Brightly

Rock, rock, rock, oh, ba - by. Rock, rock, rock oh, ba - by.

To Coda ⊕

Rock, rock, rock, oh, ba - by. Rock, rock, rock, oh, ba - by...

Verse

1. Rock and roll is here to stay,___ and it will nev - er die.___
3. *See additional lyrics*

It was meant to be that way,___ though I don't know why.___

I don't care what peo - ple say,___ rock and roll is here to stay!___

We don't care what peo - ple say,___ rock and roll is here to stay.___

Verse

2., 4. Rock and roll will al - ways be,___ I dig it to the end.___

Rocket 88

Words and Music by Jackie Brenston

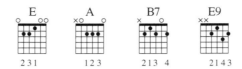

Strum Pattern: 1, 3
Pick Pattern: 3, 5

Intro
Moderately fast (♫ = ♩♪)

To Coda 3 ⊕

To Coda 1 ⊕

Verse

1. You wom-en have heard of jal-op-ies, you've heard the
3. *See additional lyrics*

noise they make. But let me in-tro-duce my new Rock-et eight-y eight. Yes,

it's straight, just won't wait, ev-'ry-bod-y likes my Rock-

et eight - y eight. Ba - by, we'll ride in style, __ mov - in' all __ a - long.

D.S. al Coda 1   ⊕ **Coda 1**   **Verse**

__   2. V - eight mo - tor 'n' this smart __

__ 'n' de - sign, black con - vert - a - ble top __ an' the gals __ don't __ mind. __

Sport - in' with me, __ rid - in' all __ 'round __ town __ for joy. __   Blow your horn,

D.S. al Coda 2   ⊕ **Coda 2**   *D.S. al Coda 3*

Ray - mond, blow it!

⊕ **Coda 3**

Additional Lyrics

3. Step in my Rocket and don't be late,
   Baby, we're pullin' out about half past eight.
   Goin' 'round the corner and get a fifth.
   Ev'rybody, my car's gonna take a little nip.
   Move on out, boozin' 'n' cruisin' along.

Runaway

Words and Music by Del Shannon and Max Crook

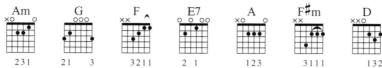

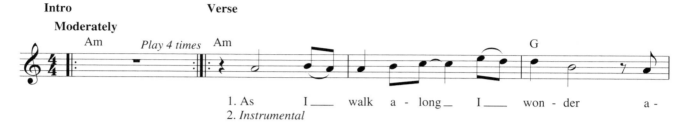

Strum Pattern: 4, 3
Pick Pattern: 3, 4

1. As I walk a - long I wonder a-
2. *Instrumental*

what went wrong with our love a love that was so strong.

And as I still walk on I

think of the things we've done to - geth - er a-

while our hearts were young. I'm a - walk - in'

in the rain. Tears are fall - in' and I feel the pain.

A - wish - in' you were here by me to end this

mis - er - y. And I won - der, I wo - wo - wo - wo -

won - der why, a - why, why, why, why,

why she ran a - way, and I won - der

a - where she will stay, my lit - tle run - a - way, a -

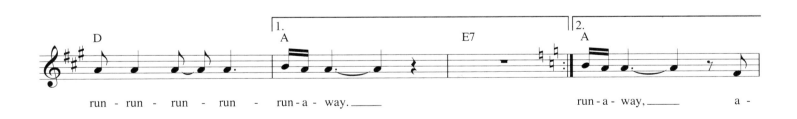

run - run - run - run - run - a - way. run - a - way, a -

Outro *Repeat and fade*

run - run - run - run - run - a - way. Run - run - run - run - run -

Save the Last Dance for Me

Words and Music by Doc Pomus and Mort Shuman

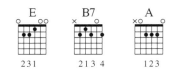

Strum Pattern: 2
Pick Pattern: 4

1. You can dance ev-'ry dance with the guy who gives
2., 3. *See additional lyrics*

___ you the eye; let him hold you tight. ___ You can

smile ___ ev-'ry smile for the man who held ___ your hand ___ 'neath the

pale moon-light. ___ {1., 2. But / 3. 'Cause} don't for-get who's tak-ing you home ___

___ and in whose arms you're gon-na be. So dar-lin', save the

last dance ___ for ___ me. Mm. ___   2. Oh, I   me. Mm.

Bridge

1. Ba - by, don't you know I love you so?___ Can't you feel it when we
2. *Instrumental*

touch? I will nev - er, nev - er let you go.___

To Coda ⊕   *D.S. al Coda* **(take 2nd ending)**

I love you, oh, so___ much. 3. You can

⊕ **Coda**   **Chorus**

'Cause don't for - get who's tak - ing you home___ and in whose arms you're

gon - na be. So, dar - lin', save the

last dance___ for___ me. Mm.___

Outro   *Repeat and fade*

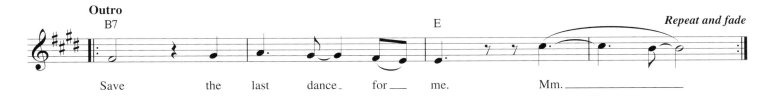

Save the last dance___ for___ me. Mm.___

Additional Lyrics

2. Oh, I know that the music's fine
   Like sparkling wine; go and have your fun.
   Laugh and sing, but while we're apart
   Don't give your heart to anyone.

3. You can dance, go and carry on
   Till the night is gone and it's time to go.
   If he asks if you're all alone,
   Can he take you home, you must tell him no.

Sea of Love

Words and Music by George Khoury and Philip Baptiste

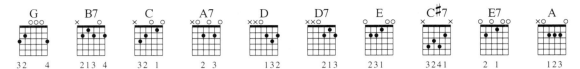

Strum Pattern: 9
Pick Pattern: 9

Verse

1., 3. Do you re - mem - ber_ when_ we met? That's the day_____ I
2. *See additional lyrics*

knew you were my pet. I_____ want to tell you_ how_ much_ I

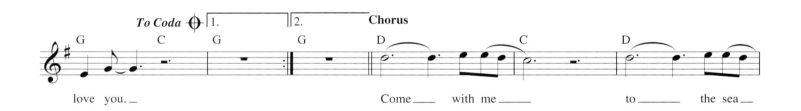

love you. _ Come_____ with me_____ to_____ the sea_

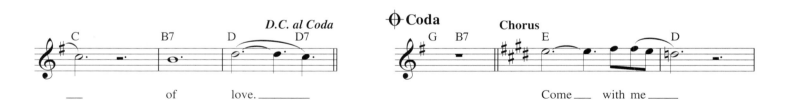

_ of love. _____ Come_ with me_

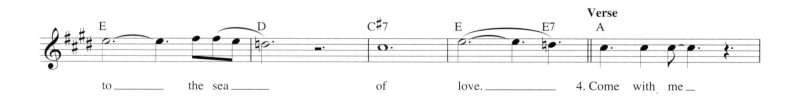

to_____ the sea_____ of love. _____ 4. Come with me_

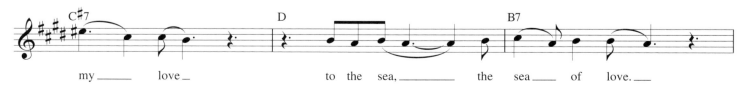

my_____ love_ to the sea,_____ the sea of love._____

I ___ want to tell you just how ___ much I love you. ___

I ___ want to tell you, oh, ___ how much ___ I love you. ___

Additional Lyrics

2. Come with me my love
   To the sea, the sea of love.
   I want to tell you
   Just how much I love you.

Sh-Boom
(Life Could Be a Dream)

Words and Music by James Keyes, Claude Feaster, Carl Feaster, Floyd McRae and James Edwards

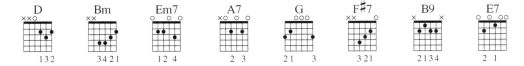

Strum Pattern: 3, 4
Pick Pattern: 3, 4

Hey, non - ny ding dong, a -

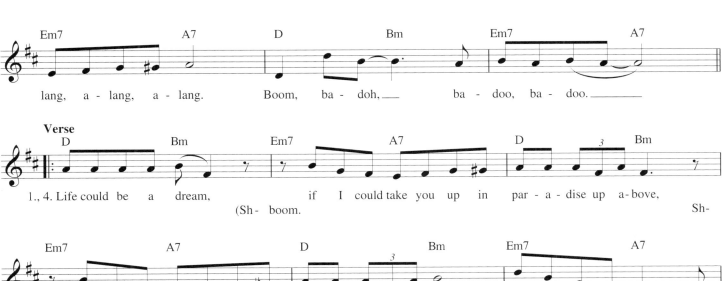

lang, a - lang, a - lang.   Boom, ba - doh, ___ ba - doo, ba - doo. ___

1., 4. Life could be a dream, if I could take you up in par - a - dise up a - bove, Sh-
(Sh - boom.

if you would tell me I'm the on - ly one that you love, life could be a dream, sweet-
boom.)

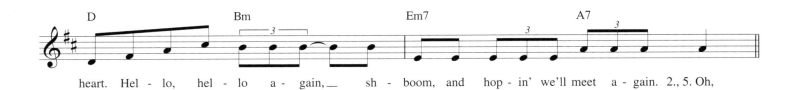

heart. Hel - lo, hel - lo a - gain, __ sh - boom, and hop - in' we'll meet a - gain. 2., 5. Oh,

Verse

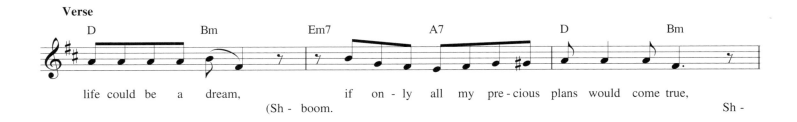

life could be a dream, if on - ly all my pre - cious plans would come true, Sh -
(Sh - boom.

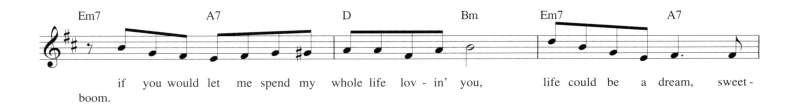

if you would let me spend my whole life lov - in' you, life could be a dream, sweet -
boom.

% **Bridge**

heart. _____ Ev - 'ry time I look at you __

some - thing is on my mind. __ If you'd do what I

want you to, ____ ba - by, we'd be so fine. ____ 3., 6., 7. Oh,

Verse

life could be a dream, if I could take you up in par - a - dise up a - bove, Sh -
(Sh - boom.

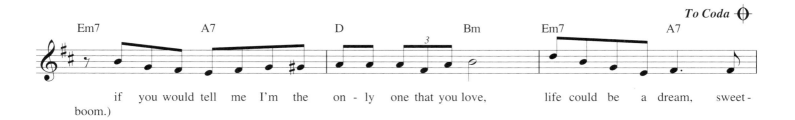

To Coda ⊕

if you would tell me I'm the on - ly one that you love, life could be a dream, sweet -
boom.)

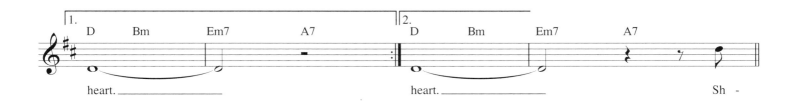

1. heart.

2. heart. Sh -

Interlude

boom, sh - boom, ya, da, da, da, da, da, da, da, da, da. Sh -

boom, sh - boom, ya, da, da, da, da, da, da, da, da, da. Sh -

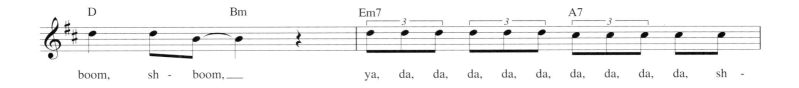

boom, sh - boom, ya, da, da, da, da, da, da, da, da, da, sh -

1. boom.

2. Sh - boom.

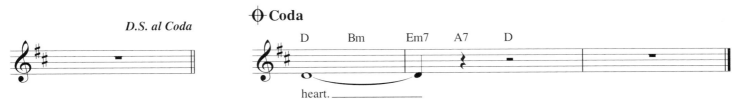

D.S. al Coda

⊕ **Coda**

heart.

See You Later, Alligator

Words and Music by Robert Guidry

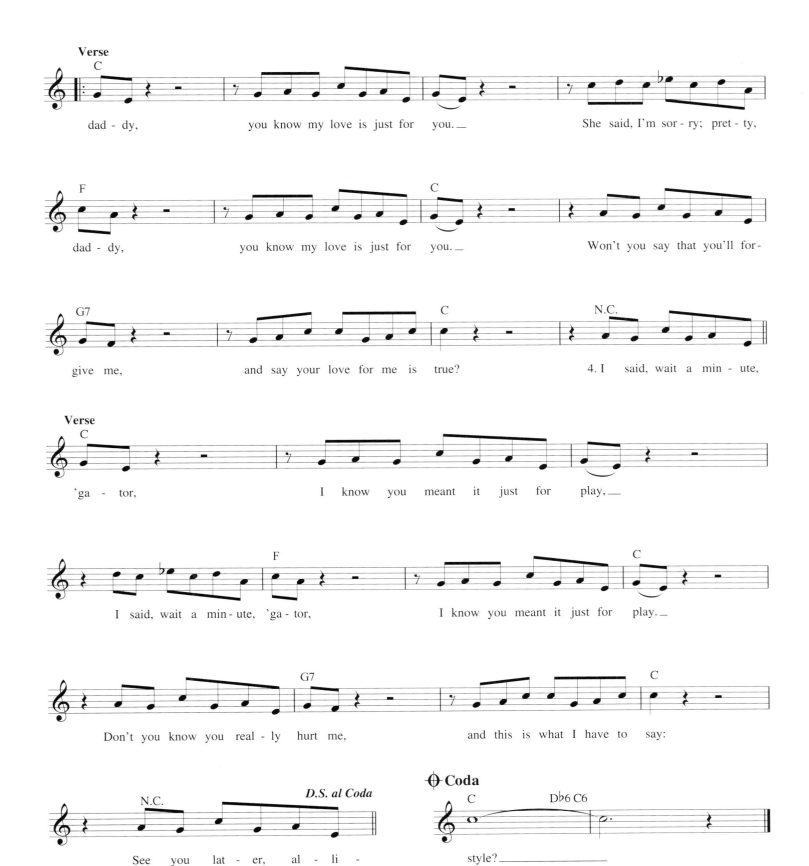

Additional Lyrics

2. When I thought of what she told me,
Nearly made me lose my head.
When I thought of what she told me,
Nearly made me lose my head.
But the next time that I saw her,
Reminded her of what she said.

Shake, Rattle and Roll

Words and Music by Charles Calhoun

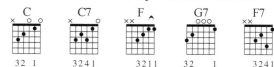

Strum Pattern: 2
Pick Pattern: 2

Moderately **Verse**

1. Get out ____ from that kitch - en and rat - tle those pots and pans. ____
2., 3., 4. *See additional lyrics*

Get out ____ from that kitch - en and rat - tle those pots and pans; ____

well, roll my break - fast, 'cause ____ I'm a hun - gry man. ____

Chorus

Shake, rat - tle and roll, ____ shake, rat - tle and roll, ____

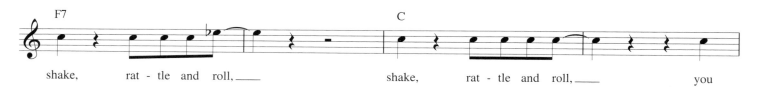

shake, rat - tle and roll, ____ shake, rat - tle and roll, ____ you

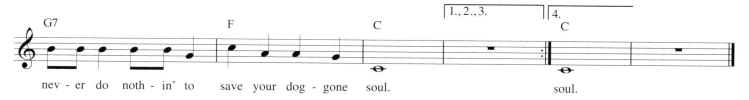

nev - er do noth - in' to save your dog - gone soul. soul.

Additional Lyrics

2. Wearin' those dresses, your hair done up so right.
   Wearin' those dresses, your hair done up so right;
   You look so warm, but your heart is cold as ice.

3. I'm like a one-eyed cat, peepin' in a seafood store.
   I'm like a one-eyed cat, peepin' in a seafood store;
   I can look at you, tell you don't love me no more.

4. I believe you're doing me wrong and now I know.
   I believe you're doing me wrong and now I know;
   The more I work, the faster my money goes.

Sixteen Candles

Words and Music by Luther Dixon and Allyson R. Khent

Strum Pattern: 2
Pick Pattern: 5

Shop Around

Words and Music by Berry Gordy and William "Smokey" Robinson

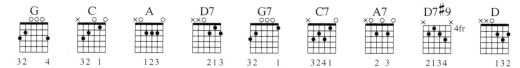

Strum Pattern: 3, 4
Pick Pattern: 4, 5

Intro
Freely

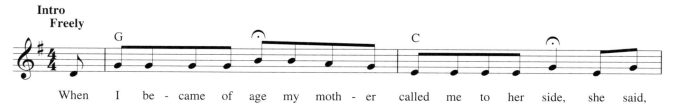

When I be - came of age my moth - er called me to her side, she said,

"Son, you're grow - ing up now, pret - ty soon you'll take a bride." 1. And then she

Verse
Moderately bright

said, "Just be - cause you've be - come a young man now, there's still some things that you
2. *See additional lyrics*

don't un - der - stand now; be - fore you ask some girl for her hand, now, _____

keep your free - dom for as long as you can now." My ma - ma told

me, "You bet - ter shop a - round, oh yeah, you bet - ter shop a - round." (Shop, shop a -

round.) 2. "Ah, _____ round.) "A try to get your - self a bar - gain son. _____

Don't be sold___ on the ver-y first one._____ A pret-ty girls come a

dime a doz-en, a try to find one who's gon-na give you true___ lov-in'."___

Verse

3., 4. "Be-fore you take a girl and say I do___ now, make sure she's in

To Coda

love with a you now." My ma-ma told me, "You bet-ter shop a-

Interlude

Play 3 times

round."

D.S. al Coda

Coda

Oo,_____ yeah._____ "Make sure that her love is true___ now.

I hate to see you feel-in' sad___ and blue now."___ My ma-ma told me, "You bet-ter shop a-

Outro

w/ Voc. ad lib.

Repeat and fade

round." (Shop a - round.) (Shop a - round.)

Additional Lyrics

2. "Ah, there's some things that I want you to know now:
Just as sure as the wind's gonna blow now,
Women come and the women gonna go now;
Before you tell 'em that you love them so now..."
My mama told me, "You better shop around,
Oh yeah, you better shop around."

Shout

Words and Music by O'Kelly Isley, Ronald Isley and Rudolph Isley

Strum Pattern: 2, 3
Pick Pattern: 4, 5

leave ___ me ___ I don't want no - bod - y else, hey, hey.

I said I want you to know, _____ hey. I said I want you to know ___

($\flat$ = $\flat$)　　　　　　　　　　　　　　　　　　　　　　　*D.S. al Coda*

___ right now, yeah, yeah. You know you make me wan - na

Coda

Freely

C　N.C.　　　　　　　　　　　　　　　　　　　　* C

(Shout!)　Now wait _____ a min - ute. I feel

* One strum per chord, next 11 meas.

F/C　　　　　　　　　　　　┌─ 3 ─┐　　　　C　F/C　　C

all _____ right. ___

　　　　　　　　　　　　　　　　(Yeah, yeah, yeah, yeah, yeah,

　　　　　　　　　　C7　　　　　　　　　　　┌─ 3 ─┐

Now that I've got my wom - an, I feel all _____

yeah.)

F7

right. ___　　　　　Ev - 'ry time I think a - bout you. You been so good to me.

(Yeah, yeah, yeah, yeah, yeah.)

A tempo　　　　　　**Chorus**
　　　　　　　　　　　C　　　　　　　　　　　　Am

You know you make me wan - na (Shout!) lift my hands up and (Shout!) throw my head back and

C　　　　　　　　　　Am　　　　　　　　　C

(Shout!) pick my hands up and (Shout!) come on ___ now. (Shout!) Take it eas - y.

126

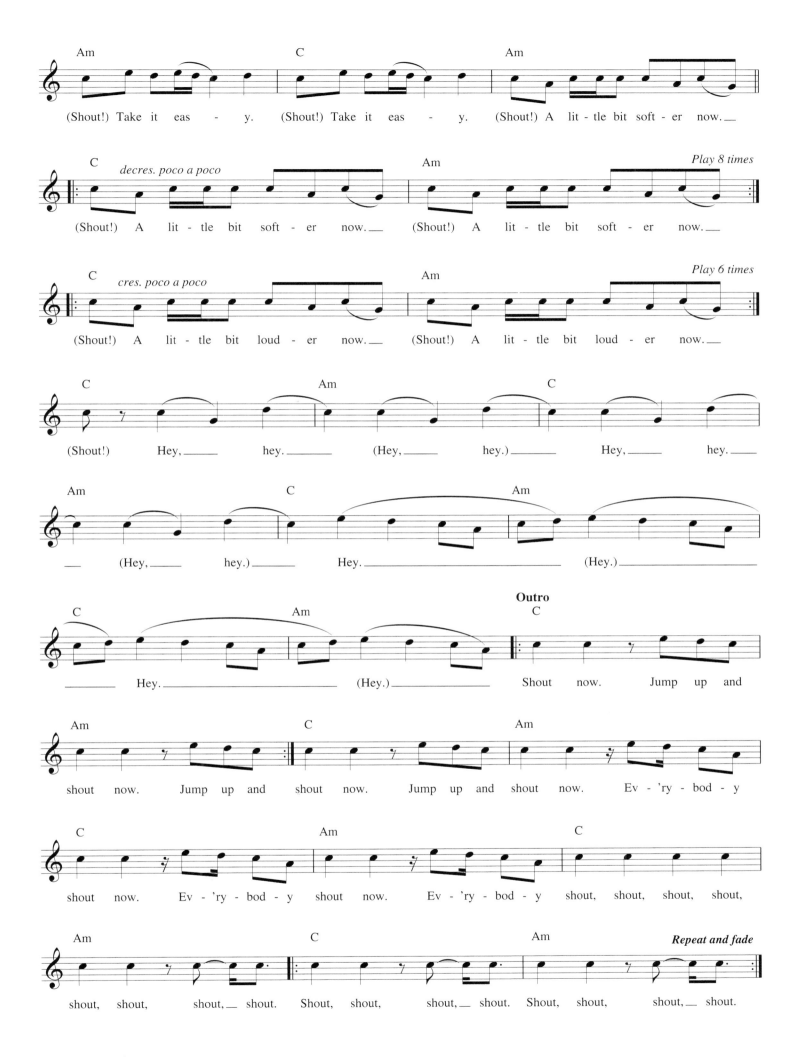

Sleepwalk

By Santo Farina, John Farina and Ann Farina

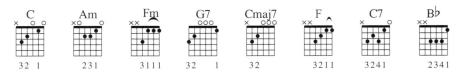

Strum Pattern: 8
Pick Pattern: 8

Susie-Q

Words and Music by Dale Hawkins, Stan Lewis and Eleanor Broadwater

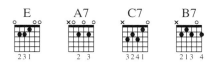

Strum Pattern: 3
Pick Pattern: 3

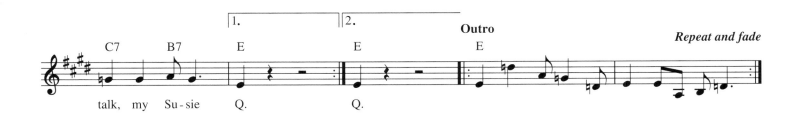

Additional Lyrics

2. Well, say that you'll be true.
Well, say that you'll be true.
Well, say that you'll be true.
And never leave me blue,
My Susie Q.

Splish Splash

Words and Music by Bobby Darin and Murray Kaufman

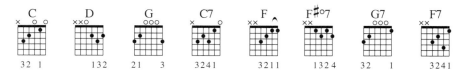

Strum Pattern: 2
Pick Pattern: 4

1. Splish splash, I was tak - in' a bath
2. *See additional lyrics*

long a - bout a Sat - ur - day night. A rub dub, just re -

lax - in' in the tub, think - in' ev - 'ry - thing was al - right. Well, I

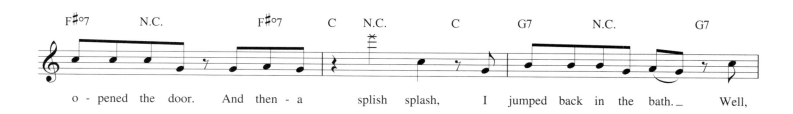

stepped out the tub, I put my feet on the floor, I wrapped the towel a - round me and I

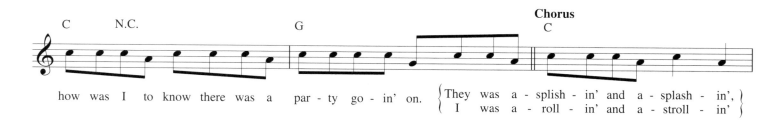

o - pened the door. And then - a splish splash, I jumped back in the bath. Well,

how was I to know there was a par - ty go - in' on. { They was a - splish - in' and a - splash - in', I was a - roll - in' and a - stroll - in' }

reel - in' with the feel - in', mov - in' and a - groov - in', { rock - in' and a - roll - in'. }
{ splish - in' and a - splash - in'. }

Saxophone Solo

F7　　　　　　　　　　　　　　　　　　　　C　　　　　　　　　　　　　G

Yeah! __

F　　　　　　　　C　　　　　　　1. G　　　N.C.　　　2. G

Yes, _____ I was a -

𝄋 **Chorus**

C

{ splish - in' }
{ Splish - in' } and a - splash - in', I was a - roll - in' and a - stroll - in'.

F7

Yeah, __ I was a - mov - in' and a - groov - in'. Woo! We was a -

C　　　　　　　　　　　　　　　　　　　　　　　G

reel - in' and a - stroll - in'. Ha! We was a - roll - in' and a - stroll - in',

F　　　　　　　　　　　　　　　　C　　　　　　　　　　　*D.S. and fade*

mov - in' with the groov - in'. Splish splash. Yeah. Mm.

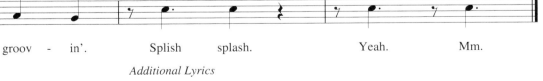
Additional Lyrics

2. Bing bang, I saw the whole gang
   Dancin' on my livin' room rug. Yeah!
   Flip flop, they was doin' the bop,
   All the teens had the dancin' bug.
   There was Lollipop a-with-a Peggy Sue.
   Good golly, Miss Molly was-a even there too.
   A-well-a splish splash, I forgot about the bath.
   I went and put my dancin' shoes on, yeah.

Tears on My Pillow

Words and Music by Sylvester Bradford and Al Lewis

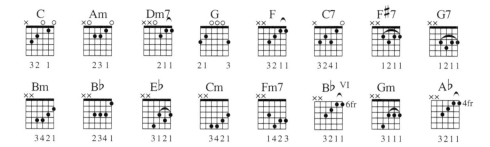

Strum Pattern: 8
Pick Pattern: 8

Bridge

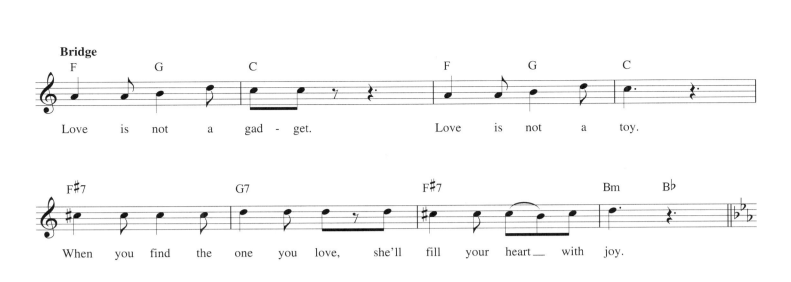

Love is not a gad - get. Love is not a toy.

When you find the one you love, she'll fill your heart___ with joy.

Verse

3. If we could start a - new, ___ I ___ would - n't hes - i - tate. ___

I'd ___ glad - ly take you back ___ and ___ tempt the

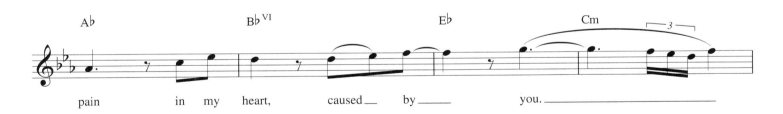

hand of fate. ___ Tears ___ on my pil - low,

pain in my heart, caused ___ by ___ you. ___

Outro   *Repeat and fade*

Fm7   B♭VI   E♭   Cm   Fm7   B♭VI

Additional Lyrics

2. If we could start anew,
   I wouldn't hesitate.
   I'd gladly take you back
   And tempt the hand of fate.
   Tears on my pillow,
   Pain in my heart, caused by you.

Teen Angel

Words and Music by Jean Surrey

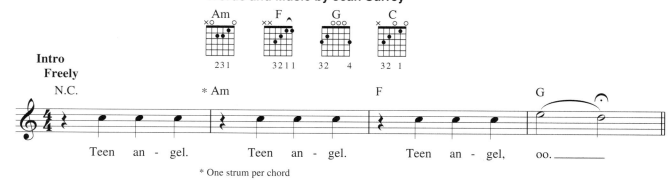

Teen an-gel. Teen an-gel. Teen an-gel, oo.

* One strum per chord

1. That fate-ful night the car was stalled up-on the rail-road track.
2., 3. *See additional lyrics*

* *sim.,* next 6 meas.

Strum Pattern: 4
Pick Pattern: 3, 4

I pulled you out and we were safe, but you went run-ning back.

Teen an-gel, can you hear me? Teen an-gel, can you see me? Are you some-where up a-bove, and am I still your own true love?

* Use Pattern 10

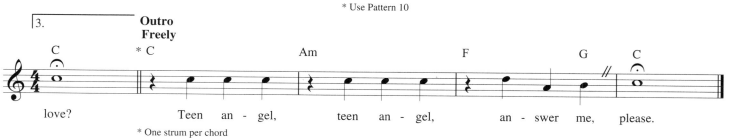

love? Teen an-gel, teen an-gel, an-swer me, please.

* One strum per chord

Additional Lyrics

2. What was it you were looking for
That took your life that night?
They said they found my high school ring
Clutched in your fingers tight.

3. Just sweet sixteen and now you're gone;
They've taken you away.
I'll never kiss your lips again;
They buried you today.

That'll Be the Day

Words and Music by Jerry Allison, Norman Petty and Buddy Holly

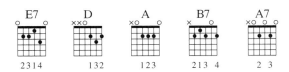

Strum Pattern: 1
Pick Pattern: 2

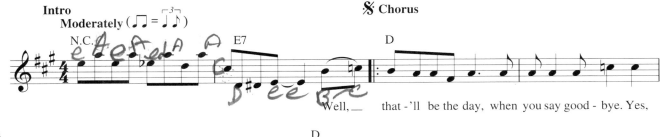

Well,___ that-'ll be the day, when you say good - bye. Yes,

that -'ll be the day, when you make me cry. You say you're gon - na leave, you know it's a lie,___ 'cause

that -'ll be the day _____ when I die.___ 1. Well, you give me all your lov - in' and your
2. *See additional lyrics*

tur - tle dov - in', a - all your hugs and kiss - es and your mon - ey too.___ Well,___ a-

you know you love me ba - by, still ___ you tell me, may - be, that some - day, well, I'll be blue. Well,___

when I die.___ Well,___ that -'ll be the day, ooh. ___ That -'ll be the day,

ooh. ___ That -'ll be the day, ooh. ___ That -'ll be the day.

Additional Lyrics

2. Well, when cupid shot his dart,
   He shot it at your heart,
   So if we ever part then I'll leave you.
   You sit and hold me and you
   Tell me boldly, that some day,
   Well, I'll be through.

A Teenager in Love

Words and Music by Doc Pomus and Mort Shuman

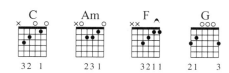

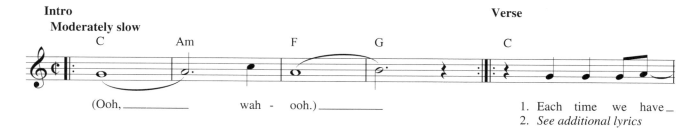

Strum Pattern: 2
Pick Pattern: 4

Intro
Moderately slow

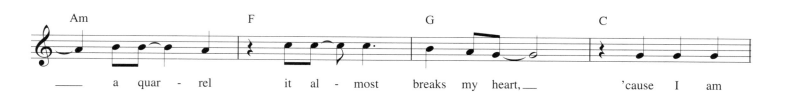

(Ooh, _____ wah - ooh.) _____

1. Each time we have _
2. *See additional lyrics*

_____ a quar - rel it al - most breaks my heart, _____ 'cause I am

so a - fraid _ that we will have _____ to part. _ Each night I

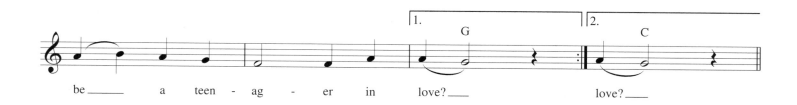

ask the stars _ up a - bove: _____ Why must I

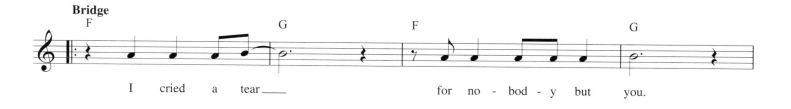

be _ a teen - ag - er in love? _ love? _

Bridge

I cried a tear _ for no - bod - y but you.

I'll be a lone - ly one __ if you should say __ we're through. 3., 4. Well,

Verse

if you want __ to make __ me cry, __ that won't be so hard __ to do. __

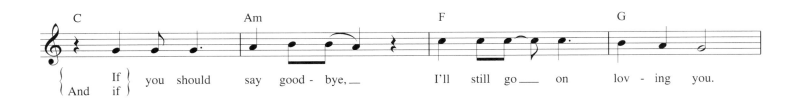

{ And If } { if } you should say good - bye, __ I'll still go __ on lov - ing you.

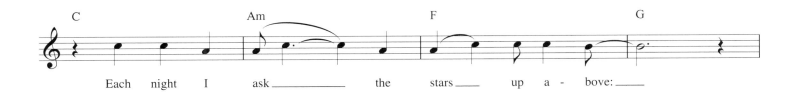

Each night I ask _____ the stars __ up a - bove: __

Why must I be __ a teen - ag - er in love? love? __

Outro

Repeat and fade

Why must I be a __ teen - ag - er in love? __

Additional Lyrics

2. One day I feel so happy;
Next day I feel so sad.
I guess I'll learn to take
The good with the bad.

Tequila

By Chuck Rio

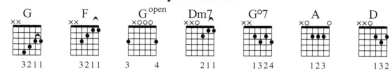

Strum Pattern: 3, 5
Pick Pattern: 3, 4

A

Moderately

* Use G open through E

3.

B

Spoken: Tequila!

Spoken: Tequila!

Travelin' Man

Words and Music by Jerry Fuller

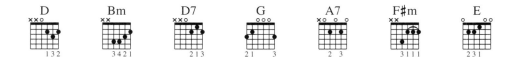

Strum Pattern: 2, 6
Pick Pattern: 4, 5

Moderate Rock

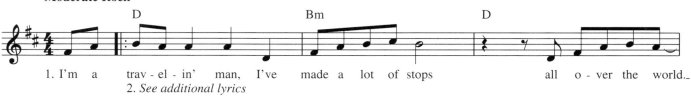

1. I'm a trav-el-in' man, I've made a lot of stops all o-ver the world.
2. *See additional lyrics*

And in ev-er-y port I own the heart of at

least one love-ly girl. 2. I've a Oh, my sweet Fräu-lein down in

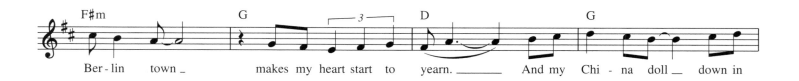

Ber-lin town makes my heart start to yearn. And my Chi-na doll down in

old Hong Kong waits for my re-turn. 3., 5. Pret-ty Pol-y-ne-sian ba-by
4. *Instrumental*

o-ver the sea, I re-mem-ber the night when we walked on the sands of

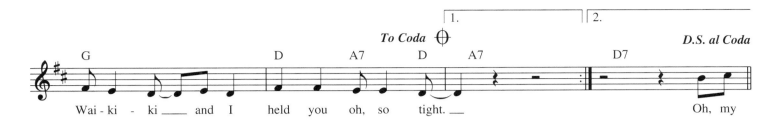

Additional Lyrics

2. I've a pretty Señorita waitin' for me
   Down in old Mexico.
   And if you're ever in Alaska, stop and see
   My cute little Eskimo.

Twist and Shout

Words and Music by Bert Russell and Phil Medley

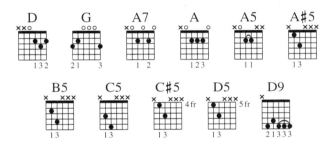

Strum Pattern: 2
Pick Pattern: 4

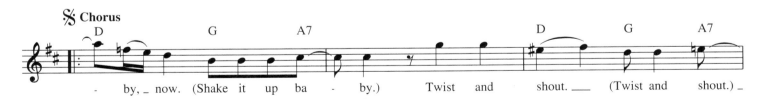

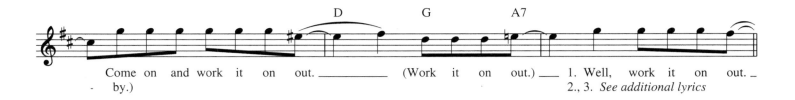

Come on and work it on out. _____ (Work it on out.) __ 1. Well, work it on out. _

\- by.) 2., 3. *See additional lyrics*

Verse

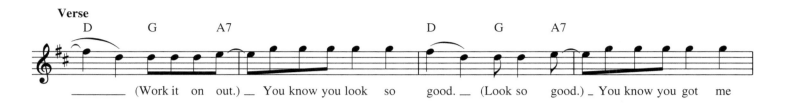

_____ (Work it on out.) _ You know you look so good. _ (Look so good.) _ You know you got me

go - in' now. (Got me goin'.) _ Just like I knew you would. _ (Like I knew you would.) _

Interlude

_____ Well, shake it up ba - ___ Ah.

D.S. al Coda

Ah. Ah. Ah. Ah. _____ Shake it up ba -

⊕ Coda   **Outro**

____ Well, shake it, shake it, shake it, ba - by, now. _ Well, shake it, shake it, shake it,

(Shake it up, ba - by.) __

ba-by, now. _ Ah. Ah. Ah. Ah.

(Shake it up, ba - by.) _

Additional Lyrics

2., 3. You know you twist, little girl, (Twist little girl.)
You know you twist so fine. (Twist so fine.)
Come on and twist a little closer now. (Twist a little closer.)
And let me know that you're mine. (Let me know you're mine.)

Tutti Frutti

Words and Music by Little Richard Penniman and Dorothy La Bostrie

Strum Pattern: 1
Pick Pattern: 2

Additional Lyrics

2. I got a gal, her name's Daisy,
   She almost drives me crazy.
   I got a gal, her name's Daisy,
   She almost drives me crazy.
   She's a real gone cookie, yes sir ree,
   But pretty little Suzy's the gal for me.

The Twist

Words and Music by Hank Ballard

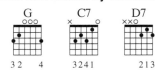

Strum Pattern: 3
Pick Pattern: 3

Verse

Moderately fast

1. Come on, ba - by, _____ let's do _____ the twist. Come on,
2., 3. *See additional lyrics*

ba - by, _____ let's do the twist. Take me by my lit - tle

hand _____ and go _____ like this. Ee, oh. Twist,

Chorus

ba - by, ba - by, twist. Just, _____
('Round and a - round and a - round and a - round.)

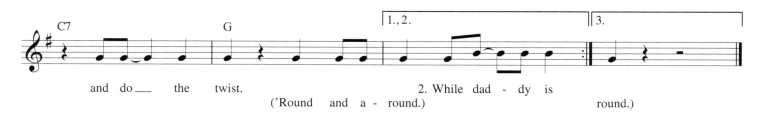

_____ just like this. Come on, _____ lit - tle miss,
('Round and a - round.)

and do _____ the twist. 2. While dad - dy is round.)
('Round and a - round.)

Additional Lyrics

2. While daddy is sleeping and mama ain't around,
   While daddy is sleeping and mama ain't around,
   We're gonna twisty, twisty, twisty
   Until we tear the house down.

3. You should see my little sis.
   You should see my little sis.
   She knows how to rock
   And she knows how to twist.

Under the Boardwalk

Words and Music by Artie Resnick and Kenny Young

Strum Pattern: 6
Pick Pattern: 4

Verse
Moderately

1. Oh, when the sun beats down __ and burns the tar up - on the roof, __
2. *See additional lyrics*
3. *Instrumental*

and your shoes get so hot you wish your ti - red feet __ were fi - re - proof. __

Chorus

Un - der the board - walk, __ down by the sea, __

yeah, __ on a blan - ket with my __ ba - by's __ where I'll __ be.

(Un-der the

Out of the sun. __ We'll be hav - in' some fun. __

board-walk. Un-der the board-walk. Un-der the

Peo - ple walk - in' a - bove. __ We'll be

board-walk. Un-der the board - walk.)

1., 2.

3.

fall - in' in love. __ Un - der the board - walk, board - walk. 2. From the walk.

Additional Lyrics

2. From the park you hear the happy sound of the carousel,
   You can almost taste the hot dogs and french fries they sell.

Up on the Roof

Words and Music by Gerry Goffin and Carole King

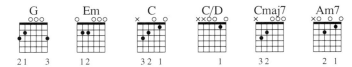

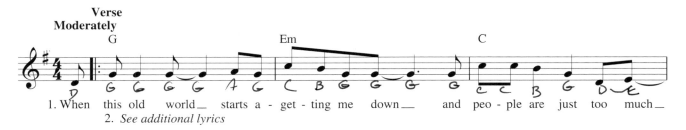

Strum Pattern: 4, 6
Pick Pattern: 4, 6

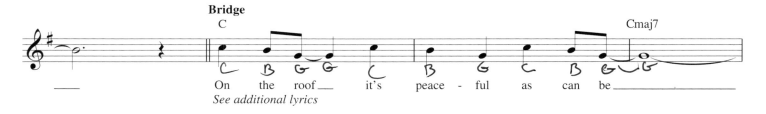

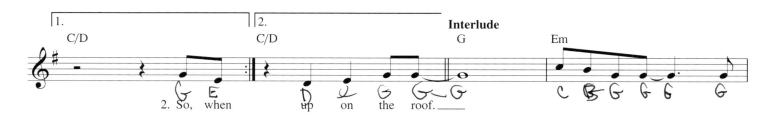

Additional Lyrics

2. So, when I come home feelin' tired and beat,
   I'll go up where the air is fresh and sweet.
   I'll get far away from the hustling crowds
   And all that rat race noise down in the street.

Bridge   On the roof that's the only place I know
   Where you just have to wish to make it so;
   Up on the roof.

Wake Up Little Susie

Words and Music by Boudleaux Bryant and Felice Bryant

Strum Pattern: 1
Pick Pattern: 1

Additional Lyrics

3. The movie wasn't so hot.
   It didn't have much of a plot.
   We fell asleep, our goose is cooked,
   Our reputation is shot.
   Wake up, little Susie.
   Wake up, little Susie.

Walk Don't Run

By Johnny Smith

Strum Pattern: 1, 2
Pick Pattern: 4, 6

Wild Thing

Words and Music by Chip Taylor

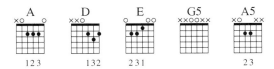

Strum Pattern: 5
Pick Pattern: 1

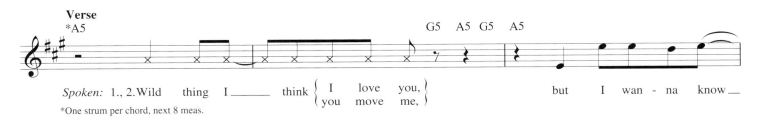

Why Do Fools Fall in Love

Words and Music by Morris Levy and Frankie Lymon

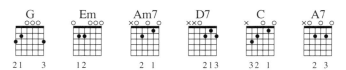

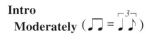

Strum Pattern: 3
Pick Pattern: 3

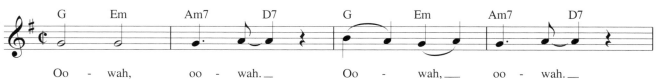

Intro
Moderately

Oo - wah, oo - wah. ___ Oo - wah, ___ oo - wah. ___

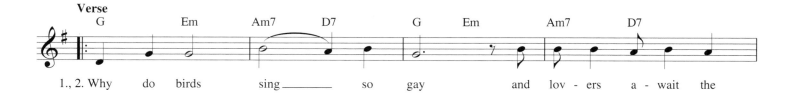

Oo - wah, ___ oo - wah. ___ Why do fools ___ fall in love? ___

Verse

1., 2. Why do birds sing _____ so gay and lov - ers a - wait the

break of day? Why do they fall in love? _____

Why does the rain fall from up a - bove? Why do fools

fall in love? Why do they fall in love? _____

Bridge

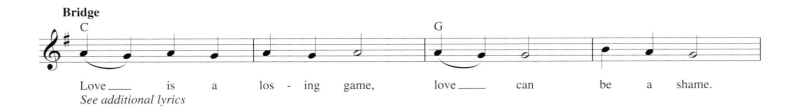

Love ___ is a los - ing game, love ___ can be a shame.
See additional lyrics

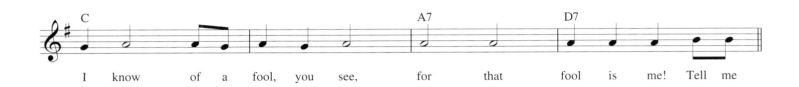

I know of a fool, you see, for that fool is me! Tell me

Outro

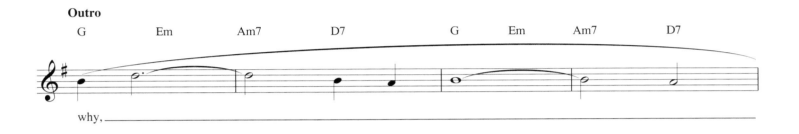

why, _____

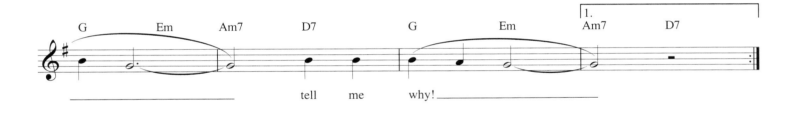

_____ tell me why! _____

Why _____ do fools

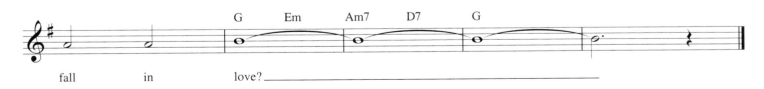

fall in love? _____

Additional Lyrics

Bridge Why does my heart skip a crazy beat?
For I know, it will reach defeat!

Wooly Bully

Words and Music by Domingo Samudio

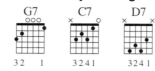

Strum Pattern: 1
Pick Pattern: 2

Pre-Intro
Moderately

Spoken: Uno, dos, one, two, tres, quattro.   Hey.   Wooly Bully. Watch it, now. Watch it.

Here he comes.   Here he comes.   Watch it, now.   He'll get you.

Verse

1. Mat - ty told Hat - ty   a - bout a thing she saw.___   Had
2., 3. *See additional lyrics*

two big horns ___   and a wool - y jaw.___ Wool - y Bul - ly, _____

___ Wool - y Bul - ly. *Spoken: Yeah, that's right.* Wool - y Bul - ly,   Wool - y

Bul - ly,   Wool - y Bul - ly.

Pre-Intro

D.S. al Coda

Coda

Outro

Spoken: He got it. He got it.

Additional Lyrics

2. Hatty told Matty
   Let's don't take no chance.
   Let's not be L 7.
   Come and learn to dance.
   Wooly Bully, Wooly Bully.
   Wooly Bully, Wooly Bully, Wooly Bully.
Spoken: Watch it, now. Watch it, watch it, watch it.

3. Matty told Hatty
   That's the thing to do.
   Get yo' someone really
   To pull the wool with you.
   Wooly Bully, Wooly Bully.
   Wooly Bully, Wooly Bully, Wooly Bully.
Spoken: Watch it, now. Watch it. Here he comes.

Ya Ya

Words and Music by Morris Levy and Clarence Lewis

Strum Pattern: 1
Pick Pattern: 3

Verse
Moderato

1. Oh well, I'm sit - tin' here, la, la, er, wait - in' for my ya, ya, uh, huh, uh

huh. Er, sit - tin' here, la, la, er, wait - in' for my ya, ya, uh huh, uh

huh. It may sound fun - ny, but I don't be - lieve she's com - in', uh huh, uh

Verse

huh. 2. Ba - by, hon - ey, __ don't leave me wor - ried, uh huh, uh huh. Er,

ba - by, hon - ey, er, don't leave me wor - ried, uh huh, uh huh. You

know that I love you. __ Oh, __ how I love you, uh huh, uh huh.

Young Blood

Words and Music by Jerry Leiber, Mike Stoller and Doc Pomus

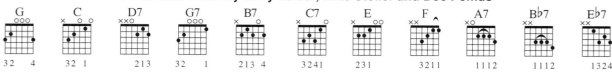

Strum Pattern: 3
Pick Pattern: 3

Verse
Moderate Rock

1. I saw her standing on the corner, ____ a yellow ribbon in her
2., 3. *See additional lyrics*

hair. I couldn't keep myself from shouting, "Look-a there, look-a there, look-a

To Coda **Chorus**

there, look-a there!" Young blood, ____ young blood, ____

young blood ____ I can't get you out of my mind. ____

Bridge

What crazy stuff, she looked so tough. I had to follow her all the way home. ____

D.C. al Coda

Then things went bad, I met her dad, he said, *Spoken:* "You better leave my daughter alone." ____

Coda **Outro-Chorus**

Young blood, ____ young blood, ____ young blood ____

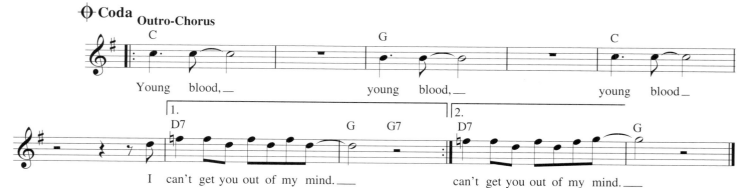

I can't get you out of my mind. ____ can't get you out of my mind. ____

Additional Lyrics

2. I took one look and I was fractured.
I tried to walk but I was lame.
I tried to talk but I just stuttered,
"What's your name, what's your name,
What's your name, what's your name?"

3. I couldn't sleep a wink for trying.
I saw the rising of the sun.
And all night long my heart was crying,
"You're the one, you're the one,
You're the one, you're the one!"

THE BOOK SERIES
FOR EASY GUITAR

THE BEATLES BOOK
An incredible collection of 100 Beatles' favorites arranged for easy guitar, including: Across the Universe • All My Loving • And I Love Her • Baby You're a Rich Man • The Ballad of John and Yoko • Birthday • Drive My Car • Eleanor Rigby • Good Day Sunshine • Helter Skelter • Here Comes the Sun • Hey Jude • I Saw Her Standing There • I'll Follow the Sun • Lady Madonna • Michelle • Penny Lane • Revolution • Twist and Shout • Yesterday • and more.
00699266 Easy Guitar $19.95

THE BLUES BOOK
84 super blues tunes: All Blues • Baby Please Don't Go • Double Trouble • Fine and Mellow • Honest I Do • I'm Your Hoochie Coochie Man • Killing Floor • Love Struck Baby • Mean Old World • Milk Cow Blues • Pinetop's Blues • Route 66 • See See Rider • Statesboro Blues • Texas Flood • Trouble in Mind • Who Do You Love • more.
00702104 Easy Guitar $15.95

THE BROADWAY BOOK
93 unforgettable songs from 57 shows! Includes: Ain't Misbehavin' • Beauty and the Beast • Cabaret • Camelot • Don't Cry for Me Argentina • Edelweiss • Hello, Dolly! • I Could Write a Book • I Whistle a Happy Tune • Mame • My Favorite Things • One • People • September Song • Some Enchanted Evening • Tomorrow • Try to Remember • Where or When • more.
00702015 Easy Guitar $17.95

THE ERIC CLAPTON BOOK
83 favorites from this guitar legend, including: After Midnight • Badge • Bell Bottom Blues • Change the World • Cocaine • I Can't Stand It • I Shot the Sheriff • Lay Down Sally • Layla • Let It Rain • Pretending • Strange Brew • Tears in Heaven • White Room • Wonderful Tonight • more.
00702056 Easy Guitar $17.95

THE CLASSIC COUNTRY BOOK
101 country classics: Act Naturally • Cold, Cold Heart • Could I Have This Dance • Crazy • Daddy Sang Bass • D-I-V-O-R-C-E • El Paso • Folsom Prison Blues • The Gambler • Heartaches by the Number • I Fall to Pieces • I'm Not Lisa • King of the Road • Kiss an Angel Good Mornin' • Lucille • Mississippi Woman • Rocky Top • Sixteen Tons • Son-of-a-Preacher Man • When Two Worlds Collide • Will the Circle Be Unbroken • You Needed Me • more.
00702018 Easy Guitar $19.95

THE CLASSIC ROCK BOOK
89 huge hits: American Woman • Beast of Burden • Black Magic Woman • Born to Be Wild • Cocaine • Dust in the Wind • Fly Like an Eagle • Free Bird • Gimme Three Steps • I Can See for Miles • Iron Man • Layla • Magic Carpet Ride • Nights in White Satin • Reelin' in the Years • Revolution • Roxanne • Sweet Home Alabama • Walk This Way • You Really Got Me • and more.
00698977 Easy Guitar $19.95

Visit Hal Leonard Online at
www.halleonard.com

Prices, contents, and availablilty subject to change without notice.

THE DISNEY SONGS BOOK
A comprehensive collection of 73 classic and contemporary Disney favorites arranged for easy guitar, including: Beauty and the Beast • Can You Feel the Love Tonight • Candle on the Water • Chim Chim Cher-ee • Feed the Birds • Friend Like Me • Hakuna Matata • I'm Late • It's a Small World • Mickey Mouse March • The Siamese Cat Song • A Spoonful of Sugar • Supercalifragilisticexpialidocious • Under the Sea • A Whole New World • Winnie the Pooh • You'll Be in My Heart (Pop Version) • You've Got a Friend in Me • more.
00702168 Easy Guitar $19.95

THE FOLKSONGS BOOK
Over 133 classic folk songs in easy guitar format. Songs include: Alouette • Blow the Man Down • The Blue Tail Fly (Jimmy Crack Corn) • Danny Boy • For He's a Jolly Good Fellow • I've Been Working on the Railroad • Man of Constant Sorrow • On Top of Old Smoky • Scarborough Fair • Sometimes I Feel Like a Motherless Child • This Old Man • Wabash Cannon Ball • When the Saints Go Marching In • Yankee Doodle • more.
00702180 Easy Guitar $14.95

THE GOSPEL SONGS BOOK
A virtual bible of gospel songs arranged for easy guitar. Features: Amazing Grace • At Calvary • Blessed Assurance • Church in the Wildwood • He Touched Me • His Eye Is on the Sparrow • How Great Thou Art • I Love to Tell the Story • I Saw the Light • Just a Closer Walk with Thee • More Than Wonderful • The Old Rugged Cross • Rock of Ages • Shall We Gather at the River? • Sweet by and By • Turn Your Radio On • Will the Circle Be Unbroken • and more.
00702157 Easy Guitar $14.95

THE HYMN BOOK
An inspirational collection of 143 glorious hymns arranged for easy guitar. Includes: Abide with Me • Amazing Grace • At the Cross • Be Thou My Vision • Blessed Assurance • Come, Thou Fount of Every Blessing • Fairest Lord Jesus • Holy, Holy, Holy • Just a Closer Walk with Thee • Nearer, My God, to Thee • The Old Rugged Cross • Rock of Ages • more. Perfect for church services, sing-alongs, bible camps and more!
00702142 Easy Guitar $14.95

THE JAZZ STANDARDS BOOK
100 standard songs in easy guitar format. Songs include: Ain't Misbehavin' • Always • Autumn in New York • Blue Skies • Come Rain or Come Shine • Fly Me to the Moon (In Other Words) • Georgia on My Mind • God Bless' the Child • I Didn't Know What Time It Was • I've Grown Accustomed to Her Face • In a Sentimental Mood • It Don't Mean a Thing (If It Ain't Got That Swing) • The Lady Is a Tramp • Misty • My Funny Valentine • Slightly Out of Tune (Desafinado) • Stella by Starlight • The Very Thought of You • and more.
00702164 Easy Guitar $14.95

THE LATIN BOOK
102 hot Latin tunes: Amapola • Amor Prohibido • Bésame Mucho • Brazil • Cherry Pink and Apple Blossom White • Cielito Lindo • Frenesí • Granada • Guantanamera • It's Impossible • Mambo No. 5 • Mañana • María Elena • Perfidia • Spanish Eyes • Tango of Roses • Tico Tico • Vaya Con Dios • more.
00702151 Easy Guitar $17.95

THE LOVE SONGS BOOK
100 top love songs: Always • Body and Soul • Cheek to Cheek • Cherish • Don't Know Much • Emotions • Endless Love • Feelings • Fly Me to the Moon • For All We Know • How Deep Is Your Love • La Vie En Rose • Love Me Tender • Misty • My Romance • Something • You Were Meant for Me • Your Song • more.
00702064 Easy Guitar $16.95

THE NEW COUNTRY HITS BOOK
100 hits by today's top artists! Includes: Achy Breaky Heart • Ain't Going Down ('Til the Sun Comes Up) • Blame It on Your Heart • Boot Scootin' Boogie • Chattahoochee • Down at the Twist and Shout • Friends in Low Places • Honky Tonk Attitude • Neon Moon • Somewhere in My Broken Heart • Small Town Saturday Night • T-R-O-U-B-L-E • The Whiskey Ain't Workin' • more.
00702017 Easy Guitar $19.95

THE ELVIS BOOK
100 songs from The King's career, all arranged for easy guitar, Including: All Shook Up • An American Trilogy • Are You Lonesome Tonight? • Blue Hawaii • Blue Suede Shoes • Burning Love • Can't Help Falling in Love • Don't Be Cruel (To a Heart That's True) • G.I. Blues • Good Luck Charm • Heartbreak Hotel • Hound Dog • It's Now or Never • Jailhouse Rock • Love Me Tender • Memories • Return to Sender • (Let Me Be Your) Teddy Bear • Treat Me Nice • Viva Las Vegas • and more.
00702163 Easy Guitar $19.95

THE R&B BOOK
Easy arrangements of 89 great hits: ABC • Baby I Need Your Lovin' • Baby Love • Ben • Cloud Nine • Dancing in the Street • Easy • Emotion • Exhale (Shoop Shoop) • I Heard It Through the Grapevine • I'll Be There • I'm So Excited • Man in the Mirror • My Girl • Ooo Baby Baby • Please Mr. Postman • Sexual Healing • Stand by Me • This Masquerade • Three Times a Lady • What's Going On • more.
0702058 Easy Guitar $16.95

THE ROCK CLASSICS BOOK
89 rock favorites: Back in the Saddle • Bennie and the Jets • Day Tripper • Evil Ways • For Your Love • Free Ride • Hey Joe • Juke Box Hero • Killer Queen • Low Rider • Oh, Pretty Woman • Pride and Joy • Ramblin' Man • Rhiannon • Smoke on the Water • Young Americans • more.
00702055 Easy Guitar $17.95

THE WEDDING SONGS BOOK
This collection contains easy arrangements for 94 songs of love and devotion appropriate for performance at weddings. Includes: Always • Endless Love • Grow Old with Me • I Will Be Here • Just the Way You Are • Longer • My Romance • Ode to Joy • This Very Day • Valentine • Wedding March • When You Say Nothing at All • A Whole New World • and many more!
00702167 Easy Guitar $16.95

FOR MORE INFORMATION, SEE YOUR LOCAL MUSIC DEALER,
OR WRITE TO:

HAL•LEONARD®
CORPORATION
7777 W. BLUEMOUND RD. P.O. BOX 13819 MILWAUKEE, WI 53213

0402

EASY GUITAR
WITH NOTES & TAB

This series features simplified arrangements with notes, TAB, chord charts, and strum and pick patterns.

00702002	Acoustic Rock Hits	$12.95
00702001	Best of Aerosmith	$12.95
00702040	Best of Allman Brothers	$9.95
00702166	All-Time Best Guitar Collection	$16.95
00702169	Best of The Beach Boys	$10.95
00702143	Best Chart Hits	$8.95
00702066	Best Contemporary Hits	$9.95
00702140	Best of Brooks and Dunn	$10.95
00702095	Best of Mariah Carey	$10.95
00702043	Best of Johnny Cash	$12.95
00702033	Best of Steven Curtis Chapman	$12.95
00702073	Steven Curtis Chapman – Favorites	$10.95
00702115	Blues Classics	$10.95
00385020	Broadway Songs for Kids	$9.95
00702149	Christian Children's Songbook	$7.95
00702090	Eric Clapton's Best	$10.95
00702086	Eric Clapton from "Unplugged"	$10.95
00702016	Classic Blues	$12.95
00702141	Classic Rock	$8.95
00702053	Best of Patsy Cline	$10.95
00702170	Contemporary Christian Christmas	$9.95
00702006	Contemporary Christian Favorites	$9.95
00702091	Contemporary Country Ballads	$9.95
00702089	Contemporary Country Pickin'	$9.95
00702065	Contemporary Women of Country	$9.95
00702121	Country from the Heart	$9.95
00702145	Best of Jim Croce	$10.95
00702085	Disney Movie Hits	$9.95
00702122	The Doors	$10.95
00702041	Favorite Hymns	$9.95
00702068	Forty Songs for a Better World	$10.95
00702159	Best of Genesis	$10.95
00702174	God Bless America and Other Songs for a Better Nation	$8.95
00702057	Golden Age of Rock	$8.95
00699374	Gospel Favorites	$14.95
00702099	Best of Amy Grant	$9.95
00702113	Grease Is Still the Word	$9.95
00702160	Great American Country Songbook	$12.95
00702050	Great Classical Themes	$6.95
00702131	Great Country Hits of the '90s	$8.95
00702116	Greatest Hymns for Guitar	$7.95
00702130	The Groovy Years	$9.95
00702136	Best of Merle Haggard	$10.95
00702037	Hits of the '50s	$10.95
00702035	Hits of the '60s	$10.95
00702046	Hits of the '70s	$8.95
00702047	Hits of the '80s	$8.95
00702054	Best of Hootie and the Blowfish	$9.95
00702059	Hunchback of Notre Dame & Hercules	$9.95
00702032	International Songs	$12.95
00702045	Jailhouse Rock, Kansas City and Other Hits by Leiber & Stoller	$10.95
00702021	Jazz Standards	$14.95
00702051	Jock Rock	$9.95
00702087	New Best of Billy Joel	$10.95
00702088	New Best of Elton John	$9.95
00702162	Jumbo Easy Guitar Songbook	$19.95
00702011	Best of Carole King	$12.95
00702112	Latin Favorites	$9.95
00702097	John Lennon – Imagine	$9.95
00699003	Lion King & Pocahontas	$9.95
00702005	Best of Andrew Lloyd Webber	$12.95
00702061	Love Songs of the '50s & '60s	$9.95
00702062	Love Songs of the '70s & '80s	$9.95
00702063	Love Songs of the '90s	$9.95
00702129	Songs of Sarah McLachlan	$12.95
00702138	Mellow Rock Hits	$10.95
00702147	Motown's Greatest Hits	$9.95
00702112	Movie Love Songs	$9.95
00702039	Movie Themes	$10.95
00702117	My Heart Will Go On & Other Top Hits	$9.95
00702096	Best of Nirvana	$14.95
00702026	'90s Rock	$12.95
00702067	The Nutcracker Suite	$5.95
00699261	Oasis	$14.95
00702030	Best of Roy Orbison	$12.95
00702158	Songs from Passion	$9.95
00702125	Praise and Worship for Guitar	$9.95
00702139	Elvis Country Favorites	$9.95
00702038	Elvis Presley – Songs of Inspiration	$10.95
00702004	Rockin' Elvis	$9.95
00699415	Best of Queen	$12.95
00702155	Rock Hits for Guitar	$9.95
00702128	Rockin' Down the Highway	$8.95
00702135	Rock'n'Roll Romance	$9.95
00702092	Best of the Rolling Stones	$10.95
00702093	Rolling Stones Collection	$17.95
00702101	17 Chart Hits	$9.95
00702137	Solid Gold Rock	$9.95
00702110	The Sound of Music	$8.95
00702010	Best of Rod Stewart	$12.95
00702049	Best of George Strait	$10.95
00702042	Today's Christian Favorites	$8.95
00702124	Today's Christian Rock	$8.95
00702171	Top Chart Hits for Guitar	$8.95
00702029	Top Hits of '95-'96	$12.95
00702034	Top Hits of '96-'97	$12.95
00702007	TV Tunes for Guitar	$12.95
00702108	Best of Stevie Ray Vaughan	$10.95
00702123	Best of Hank Williams	$9.95
00702111	Stevie Wonder – Guitar Collection	$9.95

FOR MORE INFORMATION, SEE YOUR LOCAL MUSIC DEALER,
OR WRITE TO:

HAL•LEONARD®
CORPORATION

7777 W. BLUEMOUND RD. P.O. BOX 13819 MILWAUKEE, WI 53213

www.halleonard.com

0102